# I WAS ONE OF MY MEMORIES

LAURIE BLAUNER

Printed in the United States of America

First Edition
1 2 3 4 5 6 7 8 9

Cover design by David Dintenfass
Interior design by Jojo Rita and Sasha Ori

Library of Congress Cataloging-in-Publication Data

ISBN 978-1-948-587-22-8

PANK Magazine
PANK Books

To purchase multiple copies or book events, readings and author signings contact awesome@pankmagazine.com

# I WAS ONE OF MY MEMORIES

ESSAYS BY LAURIE BLAUNER

# Table of Contents

## Part I
### Time inside a Troubled Room

## Part II
### Ghost Notes

## Part III
### The Etiquette of Space

# Acknowledgements

*Cleaver Magazine* Portions of "Diary, a House"
*Connotation Press* "A Cure for Secrets"
*december* "Yesterday, Today, and Tomorrow"
*Free State Review* "Lopsided"
*Moon City Review* "We Can Talk About That"
*PANK* "I Am an Animal"
*Superstition Review* "I Was One of My Memories"
*StringTown* "Accommodations in a Lost City"
*Sycamore Review* "Time inside a Troubled Room"
*The Laurel Review* Portions of "The Adventures of Small Animals"
*Thin Air* "Uncivilization"
*Tupelo Quarterly* "Everything is Everything Else"
*What Books Press anthology called What Falls Away is Always* "Ghost Notes"
*Your Impossible Voice* "Mythomania"

Thanks to all these magazines and their dedicated editors for publishing these essays, sometimes in another version.

"We look for the oak

Who loves our company

More than other oaks."

C.D. Wright


"Houses are really bodies. We connect ourselves with walls, roofs, and objects just as we hang on to our livers, skeletons, flesh and bloodstream."

The Hearing Trumpet by Leonora Carrington


For Cyrus, of course

And many thanks to Jerry Gold, Rich Ives, and Barbara Lindsay for their help and support with the manuscript as well as Jessica Fischoff, Chris Campanioni, and everyone else at PANK books and magazine.


And to J'Lyn Chapman for choosing this manuscript. Also much appreciation to my husband, Dave, for everything.

# Part I

# Time inside a Troubled Room

# Mythomania

# I Saw My Dead Cat Everywhere

I was chronicling perceived movements through sounds, a house creaking, something falling, and a rustling wind. I credited all noises to him. Cyrus was involuntarily lunar. After sixteen years I could predict his reactions. My own animal parts expanded through his anatomy, his fur, grace, his delicate blue eyes trained on rapidly moving small objects. After he was euthanized he was suddenly gone, out of reach, but still everywhere, a trick I played on myself. I could forget his absence. It was a new year, a wet Saturday, and I missed his sense of justice. I was in a perpetual state of diminishment, which reflected my own age, which was a certain kind of emergency.

# That Meant Something

Always a new direction arrived. Everything lost weight with distance. I needed to understand living in context with ruined noises, the random, necessary exchanges with others, cloud thieves. I longed mathematically for an earlier era, one with inconveniences and causes that people died for. One where all our actions felt right but maybe weren't.

This was what I missed: the noise a live thing makes in the center of a cracking egg, the thing becoming hungry for metaphorical air, light, food, and all those intentional needs. I needed to fold my unrepeatable living into that sound and begin again at what left me here, where nothing means much, a time when I wondered at the worth of writing. Because what had happened had already happened and there was no going back or changing anything.

# Anticipating Ghosts

Both my mother and father were experienced liars. They understood the elasticity of the truth, how it could cover a large expanse or a tiny space or reach someone in waves, the large, the small, all or nothing, including everything in between. They used all of truth's various properties. They both had affairs during their almost twenty-year marriage, omitting information as they could. Then they could determine the fabricated details. One of them was more manipulative and the other one simply seemed to enjoy lying about everything as if that act could make life better.

Even now my mother will revise some family history that my sister and I will review with one another. One such myth was that she married all four of her husbands for her two daughters. I wondered if she was choosing a better self.

Some typical family lies involved when, where, with whom, age, religion, education, jobs, abuse, money, family origins, lies which, until computers became widespread, made it difficult to determine much about our background. Early on, in the carousel of lies and truth, my sister and I didn't know what we didn't know. We grew up in a compelling city, New York, and we didn't discover my mother's correct age, since she perpetually made herself younger, until she was in her eighties.

Our apartment was filled with mirrors but we couldn't really see ourselves when we looked into them. We could start over again without acknowledging our past. Both of us could begin again, right here and now.

## 1) Three Versions of Animals

1) Every day there were four patchy legs and riddles. The animal walked sideways, careful of tree roots, forgotten toys, to a calm, sunny space, lay down to sleep, waiting for what would come next.

2) My body fragmented into its parts, fur-ridden, between breathing and jumping onto things, then dashing away. I was chasing light, leaving traces, smelling history.

3) Nimble, coiled, dallying, snarling, hissing, patient, sleeping, pouncing, daubed with rain, insistent, rending, vanishing, resting, playing, appearing, gesturing, licking, ascending, descending, stalking, silent, leaving.

## 2) Three Versions of What Happened

1) I was in the library reading a book. I heard a crash outside, on the street. I blinked, lost my place and then found it again.

2) My face was open to interpretation as I was writing in my notebook. Clouds stopped and peered into the library window. Suddenly something tore at another patron's chest and he fell out of his chair, onto the floor.

3) I didn't know what to do with the morning. Last night I had refused to marry someone, then I had a dream that I had died quietly and alone in my sleep. Then I went to the library.

## Little White Lies

"Lie, lie, lie," my mother told me to make myself younger, when I was already young. When I lived with her, she wanted to be more appealing to men. I never had children, but if I had, I doubt I would ask them to do this. I would hope I had better things to do.

There are political lies, no signs of global warming, the pandemic, weapons of mass destruction, other candidates, fascist and white supremist hate groups, sleeping with women, racial inequality, birthplace disparities, money, even the size of an audience. Peeking below the surface can result in justice.

Do we lie more about what we don't understand? Or about what we do understand? Is understanding the lie?

## People Who Tell the Truth

"A part of me died in the war."
"My stories want to escape."
"I adore all my animals except for one."
"Go find your arms and legs."
"Even water wants to run away from you."
"I'm hiding under my hat."
"The world inside you is ugly."
"Your husband is lucky he found another woman."
"The edges are too sharp."
"I like drawing conclusions about everything."

## A Certain Kind of Emergency

Once I was swearing on a Bible in a Seattle court of law about something I had done that affected someone else. It concerned a detail that involved my job as a social service program coordinator.

This is a year of political elections. Lying and accusations have become indispensable. I, too, often dream of winning, the appreciation of an audience excitedly applauding me.

## What Used to Be Mine

I was always trying to correct my mistakes:
too much cheese;
unintentional insults;
a salt-filled pie;
the wrong first husband;
a state too cold to live in;
not enough exercise;
re-gifting a cup with a ceramic cat inside that you could see once you drank all the liquid. I had tired of the cup, which had been given to me for leaving my legal aid job. Often I tried to please people, but without mistakes I never get anything right.

We don't match our imagined selves.

## Lies Are Small Pieces, Torn from Ourselves, Set Adrift

Having discovered a lie I shrink away from the person who offered it. I question the reason they told it. I don't know them. I wonder why they were compelled to tell me that lie.

When I lie to myself, I don't recognize that tiny part of myself, compartmentalizing and tossing it far away from me, as if that truth had never been a part of me.

## Lie Better

Do it well. Do it very well. Believe it yourself. When asked about a car accident that had happened right in front of me, I said I didn't see anything because I didn't like the arrogant man who had been hit, but I liked the sweet, sad girl who had hit him.

My mother loved her wealthy husbands at the beginning of every marriage.

## Repeatable Living

Each day I wake with my past, generally know who I am, and sometimes the days are entirely the same and sometimes they are different. I rarely eat red meat. My body remains similar but, over time, has grown incrementally wilder and misshapen. During the insistent Seattle rain, I dance several mornings, after glimpsing far mountains over water to determine the weather. My life is quieter, I'm working less, with more reading and writing, art, movies, a cat, my husband Dave. Colors forgive me, and I worry about the red leaves on the Japanese maple trees surrounding our house. Imagination develops. I become indulgent on a limited budget. Everything is peppered with permissions and small gains. The life of the mind grows larger while my body shrinks. I'm alone often.

You'd think I would have no reason to lie.

## Animal Myths

*Native American*

Bears were humans wearing the fur of a bear. Sometimes men married them.

*Greece*

Pegasus, a winged white stallion, was a friend to the Muses, especially of poets.

*America*
Beauty and the Beast, a beautiful woman with a good-hearted but hideous man.
*Africa*
A dog brought fire to people.
*Scotland*
Silkies were sea creatures, like seals, that became human on land, married, and then returned to the sea.
*Bible*
A snake brought sin and knowledge to Adam and Eve.
*Eskimo*
A beautiful woman was actually a fox in disguise.
*Egypt*
Bastet was a cat-headed goddess of protection, love, family, and cats. Horus was a falcon-headed god of kingship and the sky.
*China*
The universe was created by a hen's egg. The yolk became the sun and sky, and the white or albumen, the earth and sea.


# Orchestra

The chorus surrounding a lie embellishes it, introduces it to other views or details or angles, can dispute a fraction of it, making it even more plausible.

"Remember when Dad broke down the back door?" my mother asked.

"He brought a crowbar and hammered away at it," I added. I thought I could hear the pounding. "He was so angry at you."

I wasn't even there.

"At least we had time to call the police," my sister, who was there, explained.

"He was so crazy," my disruptive mother stated. "I don't know why he was so mad at me about divorcing him when he was always screwing around."

Was I already a fiction writer?


# Question

Do liar's children lie more easily?


# Answer

Yes, apparently lying to your children, even with good intentions, about myths, Santa Claus or the Tooth Fairy, or to protect their feelings, makes them into liars. 88% of school-aged children fibbed after being told a falsehood in one experiment, compared to 65% who told the truth and hadn't been lied to. Children's cognitive abilities develop as they grow older and so does their capacity for mendacity, up to age fifteen, then it drops off as they go through various phases. The researchers found that lying was also linked to intelligence as well as creativity, the skill of balancing two worlds, one fictional and one real, in their heads (and knowing the difference). (*The New Republic, "Lying to Your Kids," Alice Robb, 11/11/14 and Daily Mirror, "Children who are good liars are more intelligent and have better memory skills," John Von Radowitz, 11/22/15*)

## My Lies

I'm too complicated.
My wishes aren't contaminated by your wishes.
I know what I'm doing.
I'm picking up the pieces.
I'm growing younger.
I'm comfortable doing that.
Do that again.
I can explain.

## "A Lie Gets Halfway around the World before the Truth Has a Chance to Get Its Pants On." Winston Churchill

Lying can be more fun, excluding unforeseen consequences. There's often a seed of truth within the fabrication. Is a spider deceitful when it lures an insect onto its web to be eaten? Or a snake, dragged to my door by my cat, which slinks away later? Or is it simply a matter of survival?

Is a myth a deceit or a retelling of some similar event, expanded into a bigger, more important tale?

There are messages that bypass your skin, your body. You recognize some basic needs like light or warmth and attempt to make meaning from the occurrences.

Think of a way to make everything right.
Think of a brunette ascending a snowy mountain.
Think of a snarling husband who, after he experiences happiness, stops snarling.
Think of bones threading a body.
Think of something you know, but also don't know, rising out of the lake of your gathering.

## Pretend

I once hid in my mother's New York City apartment closet to avoid a date that had arrived to pick me up. Another evening I replaced my high school, red-headed best friend for her blind date; he took me to an incredibly expensive restaurant, where, when he inquired about my brown hair, I told him that I had recently dyed it. I pretended that I didn't speak English in New York City when I didn't want to engage in conversation with someone on a bus, the subway, or the street.

Now I'm not so precise. Being older I can seem too tired and soon enough I am.

## Definition of a Lie

A difficult road, where life collects.
Someone lost in weather.
Making too much of a secret.
No, not today.

## Pathological

When I was in high school I met a teenage pathological liar. I drove him around Long Island one summer because he said he didn't have access to a car. He lied about everything, where he was going, where he had just come from, although I'd picked him up. His lying didn't seem to serve any purpose, except frustration. I was fascinated by the manner in which he caused himself continuous harm or at least discomfort or displacement for no apparent reason.

Named *pseudologia fantastica* and *mythomania* (*Wikipedia, "Pathological Lying"*) this was a disorder originally discovered by Anton Delbrueck in 1891, where a person's constant duplicity is chronic and an integral part of their personality. The cause of this compulsive behavior is currently unknown but could be environmental or genetic.

"There are no facts, only interpretations," as Nietzche once expressed.

## Perplexities

Find the lie within the lie:
If I get a diagnosis, I must have symptoms.
If I ask a question then I don't know the answer.
If I read my sister's book I comprehend what she's thinking.
If I make room for someone, they will come.
If I retrace my steps, I will find the same thing.

Does repetition make what's been said more or less false?
We can argue about it. We're communicating.
The truth is like polishing stones.
My cat isn't dead yet.
If I tell a lie, I must have chosen it.

## Representations

Fear and self-loathing. In an ad on a city bus, a beautiful woman is drenched in sunlight on a beach fringed with rocks. Disregarded, unattended children run the length of the bus. Outside, a bleak season paces itself and then gets tossed toward the sky. The attractive woman in the ad walks past perfect waves and a complacent blue sky. She is holding aloft a medication for menstrual cramps.

On television a man is gesturing; one of his feet goes forward and then another. He is talking about erectile dysfunction. His long gray hair lifts in a breeze, his tweed jacket flaps. Trees surrounding a street have husbanded around him. He is smiling, confiding in us all.

Passengers on a train are murmuring as soon as a man slumps in his seat. The train continues moving, passing a platform with a waiting area where a young woman steps forward as if to greet the train. It's an ad for a particular heart drug. The woman on the platform says to ask your doctor for this drug so that what happened to the man won't happen to you.

## What Fell from the Sky

Cyrus, my internalized cat, leaps onto our bed where sunlight is broken into geometrical patterns on the gray blanket. He lies down, purrs. I pet nonexistent fur. I kiss the air where he used to be, which is tricking me like fog to mistake one thing for another. He has become my soft religion.

## Question

Do animals lie?

## Begin Slowly

Most animals aren't consciously deceptive but they do employ certain skills, including attracting prey and repelling predators. However, some primates will hide food or use strategies to find concealed food. Cats will puff themselves up into larger cats if nervous or a mother bird will pretend to have a fatal injury in order to encourage a snake away from her babies.

Koko, the gorilla in California who had a 1,000-word signing vocabulary, loved cats and asked her keepers for a kitten. Soon after getting the kitten, Koko had a bad day and, when no one was looking, ripped a sink out from the walls of her quarters. When her humans asked her who destroyed the sink, Koko signed, "The cat did it."

## Narrative Landscape

My dead cat wanders among my good plants and bad plants, toenails clicking on our wooden floor. Soon his paws are crossed, his Siamese head resting on them. He's sleeping in another room until a noise might disturb him. I want to kidnap this other world. I'm telling myself continuous stories, in which everything can be rearranged.

My mother has different ages on different documents, driver's license, passport, and clubs. She's forgotten who she told what. These things resurface, warm and clear and leaking like balloons, which might hit something flying off into air.

## Is Omission Lying?

I could lead you first in one direction by telling you there is a famous ruin over that hill over there. I point.

I expound on its beauty, on its place in history and the importance of viewing it at least once in your lifetime.

I have forgotten to explain that it's impassable and you will never reach it since the earth is cracked deeply all around it.

You can't even see it anymore, as it has mostly disintegrated back into stones.
Only through your imagination and research can you reassemble it.
I can't help sending you off in that direction.
You will learn something, perhaps not to trust anyone.
Or you will come to see what I see, that you'll learn from the journey.
Perhaps you had once been happy.

## Where People Tell the Truth

"Of the things and people inside me, some will last."
"Animals invent their own malingering conversations."

"I am a puppet of grief."

"I don't understand what happened but I have been in this room a long time."

"You are short and round and that will eat away at your future."

"You can gather your morning into something larger."

"We are all simply waiting."

## Who Hasn't Told a Lie?

George Washington chopped down his father's favorite English cherry tree. When asked who had done such a thing by his father, the youthful George supposedly replied, "I can't tell a lie, Pa; you know I can't tell a lie. I did cut it with my hatchet."

Abraham Lincoln, Honest Abe, also supposedly claimed, "I cannot tell a lie." This quote was attributed to a financial interaction with someone in which Lincoln was overpaid and wanted to return the extra money.

These events were determined to be exaggerated dreams or myths, meant to create places for these men in history. Could these men walk away from themselves and still be remembered? (*Wikipedia, "Mason Locke Weems"*)

## More Lies

You lounge around the house waiting to be used.

You sift a path through my teeth.

You make me more into a person of my choosing.

You open more apertures inside me until nothing is left.

You are a form of denial.

You exist within neither right nor wrong but within their intricate and encompassing shadows.

You help the dead temporarily live again.

You linger in tiny boxes of anxiety.

You dance with confused intention.

Who are you?

## The Comedian of This Body

Telltale signs:

Perspiration, stuttering, strange breathing, rapid heartbeat, change in vocal tone or pitch, body or facial gestures, fidgeting, lack of eye contact, touching of conspicuous features, increased or decreased blinking, head scratching, and more head scratching.

## Unidentified Writing: As if I Am Watching Myself

When I am done with personas I abandon them like my favorite clothes. They can articulate truth through falsehoods, employ imagination in order to explain. Embellishments are part of their personalities. They are a part of me, but I'm often alarmed by something they do or say. I'm simply a conduit. Yet when personas go out for a carton of milk, I'm right there with them.

## Emergence

My longing needs facts, photographs, ashes, videos. Maybe not proof but a reenactment, as if there will be further experiences. It's hard to confine the animal within that has already been let loose. It's hard to drown again once you have been saved.

Grief walked on a leash, draped itself on my shoulders, rode across a room, had blue eyes, and expressive white paws that noisily pressed against piano keys. Grief has circled its bed, lay down upon it. Grief isn't always considered worthy of grief.

## Sequences - the Escaping Event

*The media:* An incendiary device exploded on a plane bound for New York for as yet unknown reasons.

*Young male passenger:* I was eating a peanut butter sandwich and, in my brief history, I was also waiting for my life to begin. Sky thickened and darkened outside my window. I thought perhaps I hadn't left yet.

*Older female passenger:* I wondered about the sad man sitting in front of me, disguised as a victim, hunched over his small suitcase.

*A child:* A big black balloon rose and burst and released more air than we could possibly use.

*A passenger, an actor:* I'm going to play a detective on television who, while jogging down a park path, finds body parts, three hands, a leg, a head, a sliced finger.

*Teenage passenger:* I was watching a movie about aliens who melted in sunlight. It seemed so real.

*A sick doctor on board:* I don't know how I can save anyone.

*A couple on board:* We've always liked traveling, but often we've liked the rumors about someplace better than the place we go to.

*A brother in the waiting area:* For many years my brother has made me unhappy. Now I'll finally tell him.

*Baggage handler:* I can't wait to see my friends, the poet and the gambler, tonight after work.

*The pilot:* From this distance, all the far mountains look like they're shouting. A tongue of smoke just wrapped itself around the plane.

*Woman watching the news on television:* There is a stage and an audience and actors. The stage is the world. There is real tragedy. I'm parting the curtains, but I don't really want to see.

# Consequences

"Hey, are you my father?" I asked the only person, an older man, waiting outside the Cuban restaurant in Florida, where I was visiting. He was almost seventy years old, honey-colored hair, a prominent nose, bifocals, and, as usual, smoking a cigarette. I hadn't seen him in twenty years.

Inside, we both sat at a round table with a white tablecloth, surrounded by humid air filled with the odor of spices, plantains, rice, and black beans. I asked him questions in a place I hoped he wouldn't get angry. I was already angry, nervous, and uncomfortable.

I began. "I hated it when you left New York with my sister waiting for you at your door, when you'd already gone and we didn't know where."

"I was really mad at you girls because I got you tickets for a concert and your mother had taken you out of the state and you didn't come back."

We were disputing our versions of the past and unexplained events. Leaving the state permanently, without telling anyone, even if they were divorced, seemed to trump one missed evening I didn't even recall. My sister and I were children. He was an adult. It wouldn't stay that way.

"What about that time you tried to break down the kitchen door of the apartment with a crowbar?"

"When?"

"When mom was divorcing you."

"I don't remember."

"You were yelling that it was your apartment and we had no right to change the locks."

"No, that never happened."

# Physics (Lying)

There is an empty chair you imagine filled, and a lost cat, crossing time and space. You are trying to create more stories.

## More Consequences

You love me, love me not.  You go outside.  You are inside.
I grow older and change.
One of us is a liar and the other one is a different liar.


## Possible Questions

Do you have an alibi?
Do you lie slowly or all at once?
Tell me everything you said today.  Lie.
Tell me everything you said today.  Don't lie.
What is the best lie you have told yourself?
What is the worst lie you told me?
Did you think you were only listening?
Am I still here?
Am I you yet?

# Time inside a Troubled Room

# Time inside a Troubled Room

I was looking for someone who understood, someone who took their time. Instead of bursts of light and noise talking directly to the brain, screeching colors, tasting of chocolate, the odor of lemons, sound of people speaking over one another, the touch of glass, plastic. We are sensory creatures. We need input. Our mistakes are emotional, so we bury them. Whatever is said in America these days evaporates (saved forever on our personal machines).

We're too busy for: old age; insistent messages; children; rotting weather; verb tenses; sagging relationships; vast landscapes; illness in pieces; and lurking death.

Someone, anyone, can change. The witnesses always seem right. Guns could be gentle, positive. The surface becomes everything. No diagnosis, no cure, no mystery. We invite others in but then they remind us of someone we didn't like. We see danger pooling around us. Are they trying to take things away? So what else can we do? Our vacancies are collecting inside, growing larger, clamoring. We are becoming empty. Our culture is tiring of us.

Everything sits in a mouth, held there, until it begins leaking, grows a name, a perspective.

# Benefits to Being Strangled

We are good at lists of tiny memories, unarguable mornings, fatigue stuck into a body like a knife, fights rising from potential heartbreak, money made from broken fields or torn buildings or products built from nothing, black and blue wars (inside and outside our country), big cars, hair, food, ideas. We are molded by water, by politicians with their shaky architectures. We create our own families, scarecrows in our clothes.

I am a corporation, I am Persephone, and I am asleep to the world part of the time. Some of this is my own making.

# Fragments of Sleep

In grade school, before boys, before the weight of the adult world, my closest friend had her own violent version of sleepwalking. Sometimes when I spent the night at her New York City apartment, which was full of brothers and sisters and clutter and I loved it there, she would punch or hit me in her sleep. Sometimes she pointedly wandered, successfully avoiding hazards. Every once in a while she slapped me or someone else, but I didn't like her any less.

# A Contradictory Heart

I am the opposite seasons combined. One is almost a punishment, and the other is delightful. One is ignored and avoided and the other is welcomed.

# Museum of Communications

My husband and I don't do a lot of things together. Over twenty-seven years of marriage we have different interests and memberships. My husband works occasionally at the Museum of Communications and whispers to me through ancient telephones and lines that he loves me. The equipment there has rotary dials, ringer boxes, handsets, transmitters, and magnets. I tell him I love him too on my own ruined and old equipment, and it is difficult and slow and satisfying.

But there is always someone coming. They are right in back of you, waiting. My first marriage lasted about three years, drugs, gambling, and trust issues didn't help. I waited. My second marriage is good. We are compelled to achieve without knowing why. Years ago, after I'd trapped one mouse in my Montana house and let it go outside, several more took its place.

# We Are Missing Something

I fear invitations to events I don't want to attend. Days collect, become a life, which doesn't know what will happen next within this country with its old-fashioned intentions, money, fame, power, whether we want them or not. I thought I wanted to manage my father's three bridal stores, when I was twenty years old, in college and working for my father one summer. I enjoyed brushing my fingers over the plastic-encased sparkling white sample dresses. My mother and father were getting a divorce and, for the summer, I lived with my mother. I was serious. I imagined that the strength of my future convictions would make the stores profitable and popular. My hands were busy. I cleaned, tagged, restocked, helped sell. Some of the older sales women had been in prison, had scars. Often our customers were already pregnant. My mother repeated her terrible opinions about my father: that he was sleeping with various sales women, that he stole money, that he was stupid. I tried to ignore her. But one day I heard my father upstairs, in his glass office, screaming on the telephone. When he slammed down the receiver, he yelled for me to come upstairs to his office.

"That was your mother on the phone. You're fired."

I never went back.

## There Isn't Enough Time

In Seattle, my city, motion burned through the day. The earth was disturbed and green spaces were already slipping away. Water mysteriously surrounded us and sky was dust-colored and filled with rain. I used to like being in the middle of nowhere, but nowhere is harder to find now. I'm growing older and slower, trying to revive myself, hoping for luck and culture. I like to act as if there's more time, endlessly more, but I don't want to deplete it.

## Intestinal Relations

Because of four pomegranate seeds, I alternate between heaven and hell. An irreconcilable heart waits for me on each side. The moment you take your eyes off of me, I'm gone again.

## Assembled Elsewhere

Children are lingering over their devices. We once had their attention, now children are kept busy, and we are trying to stop their bodies and minds from being shrunken into devices. Once inside them, they can visit anyone, anywhere, so we need to be vigilant about where they've been. With our devices we are never alone, almost like another face and body, and yet, as in marriage, we are lonely. We are making more of certain words, pictures, and icons and let them stand in for emotions we used to have but now simply need to project. Our children have stopped believing in anything not verified on a device, especially what's been said. Predators swirl around us. Soon the children will forget our names.

## Edith Hamilton's *Mythology*

Every year Demeter lost her only child, Persephone, for four months to the underworld, watching her die again and again. The story is about a mother's grief and the world plunged into winter, reflecting. While Persephone briefly brought back beauty in her return to her goddess mother, new green leaves, bright flowers and fruit blooming, Persephone was never the same. She had been changed because of where she had been. Persephone became "the maiden whose name may not be spoken." And, in that way, belonged to no one.

## Historical Diagnosis

We did everything for our children, the wanting and unwanting, the right to grow. I had once been good-natured. We didn't say enough to one another.

We were learning how to fix things. No one listened to me and I said the wrong things, even when talking to myself. I had been reliable. The world misled us all. In a time of war we would save the children.

## We Had Nothing in Common

Heaven and hell occupied the same world, could be different parts of the same country. I wanted to tell my husband everything since he lived in my body. I could often predict what he would do or say. He liked old electronics, music, the clarinet, our synagogue. I liked reading, writing, ballet, cats. Sometimes loneliness moved its ladder from one space to another in our house. We alternately spent time among each other's interests, jostling one person awake and then the other, a bit like Persephone.

## One of Us Was Sleeping

Hades, the king of the underworld and the dead, saw Persephone and wanted her. I had recently divorced my first husband and moved to Seattle when I met my second husband. He wanted a relationship. I wasn't ready. I was several years older. I wanted to reheat myself without commitments. I wanted to be right day after day.

The world can shrink. We can repeat our mistakes, which might also be called fate. It could conclude with something better or be replaced by something worse.

## A Country of Avoidance

Button your sweater, and it will still come undone. I laugh at the television. My family has a history of screaming and arguing with the television's points of view.

It's difficult to know what lives inside you until it's disturbed.

Things should be easier. But sometimes we wander naively into the wrong woods. A wolf appears. There are only a few paths to pursue: run, be eaten, or fight. We could be prepared, chase, fight, or eat a wolf. We would be more than ourselves. We could be the bigger wolf.

## Disposable Loneliness Myths

*Innu*

Loneliness is a longing for relatives, or people left behind, and is the worst thing that can happen, except when relatives stay too long.

*Sweden*

In Sami Shamanism Horagalles, the thunder god, is depicted as a wooden figure with a nail in his head, holding a hammer ready. That is why he is alone.

*Bible*

In the Eden of Genesis man was lonely and God created animals and then a woman. Man was still lonely.

*Italy*

Anteros was a god of love and passion who punished those who rejected the affection of others with solitude.

*Japan*

A white and yellow chrysanthemum grew side by side in a field. Lady Yellow went with an old gardener who praised her. Lady White cried bitterly. Then Lady White was discovered and brought to the palace where her happy image adorned many objects and lived forever. Lady Yellow ended up in the garbage.

*Ireland*

Female fairies swapped their deformed babies for human ones at birth. The "changeling" was only content when misfortune visited the house, with its small creepy footprints.

*Greece*

Narcissus rejected every beautiful maiden who wanted him. A goddess caused him to fall in love with himself instead. When he bent over a pool and saw his reflection, he fell in love. He wouldn't leave until he died, gazing at himself in the water. He wished he could share his story with the handsome boy in the water.

*Australia*

In Dreamtime a woman isn't allowed to marry the man she loves so she runs far away from her people. Ancestor spirits lift her into the sky world just before she dies alone. She peers down at her sad, shivering people and creates a fire in the sky for them called the sun.

*Iceland*

Huldufolk, elves and trolls, the hidden people, are often in fables warning people not to wander off from their community, putting themselves in someone else's shoes.

*France*

In 2014 a 57 year-old woman, living near Paris, who complained of "severe loneliness" and bad health, locked herself in a freezer. A fireman later discovered her frozen, curled corpse, her mouth open as though she was talking to other frozen people. *(Daily Mail, "Body of French woman suffering from 'severe loneliness' is found in her own freezer," Peter Allen, 12/2/14)*

# Effigies

I was forgetting the sequences for breaking things: deadbolts shattered, cracked windows, gangly doorknobs, familiar faces, or the previously glamorous chair. Broken highway lines between empty wild landscapes stitched through space to a wounded, taller familiar city. Everything comes from elsewhere but stays in place. (The wolves have already been here. Some of the wolves live here now.)

When my sister and I were young my mother would shut the door to our bedroom, turn off the light, and tell us not to leave or make any noise. She had a date and told him that she didn't have any children. When my mother and her date went to her bedroom, my sister and I would tiptoe through darkness into the kitchen, raid the refrigerator, and then tiptoe back to our bedroom.

Demeter, Persephone's mother, changed the land in her grief (desolate, barren) and again in her rejoicing (thick, rich, and green) depending on where her daughter resided. Both Demeter and Hades loved Persephone and she was inside them both. Both longed for her, in the same way the world makes itself ready.

We were caught up in our own lives, which was what we did to one another in a place where everyone aspired. We did the best we could with all those distractions, snow collecting in street corners like accidents, one of my friends falling into darkness, an impatient wind swirling with information from various devices. I understood traveling from inside a destination, and joy from a lack of frostbite. Where, when, why. One was leading another. I have found something else. I was always changing.

Call my name.

Then leave me behind.

# Yesterday, Today, Tomorrow

.

# Tomorrow

My face loses structure; my body is swept and reshaped as if from water, bones have the weight of rocks. I'm not sure I'm complaining; it's more of a rebuilding. While the earth is turning, gravity keeps everything from flying apart. Some of my words form more intricately and slowly and spin further away. I'm compiling my life, moment by moment.

The future continues rushing by even though I haven't arrived at the present. I often say what I mean, for better or worse. Yes, I'm a bit fragile, with a heart that resembles a fistful of red fish swishing long, red tails. I believe I need less sleep, but I sometimes feel exhausted. I like the way people, usually younger people, look through me. I can do what I want.

I have lost people's names in Seattle, this city of stray rain and bodies of water. I will be 64 soon and my mother will be 90. My mother is losing her teeth. She pockets her disorders, generally making them manageable. She tells me in her gravelly voice that she knows everything about dating, men, politics, and money, although she clings to many old-fashioned ideas about these subjects. I, on the other hand, recall and retain less as I grow older. I place my coffee cup somewhere and it is hard to find. My father died in 2001 but claimed to know very little about most things, even things that he had done.

What I can't do anymore sometimes surprises me. I'm a woman whose body is drying out and soon I'll borrow some bird's wings and collapse into myself, fly anywhere I want.

I could go to: *China*. Because of the Confucian tradition of "filial piety," elders are revered. But since industrialization, an "Elderly Rights Law" has been instituted where adult children are required to visit their parents or face a fine or jail sentence. Or *Korea*, where a 60th and 70th birthday are enormous celebrations. Or *Japan*, where 7.2% of the population will be over 80 in 2020 (compared to 4.1% in the U.S.), which may create new problems. (*The Week*, *"How the Elderly are Treated around the World,"* Karina Martinez-Carter, 7/23/13). Or *Greece*, where "old man" or "geronda" is not derogatory. Or *Montana (Native American)*, where older people have wisdom and life experiences, passed down to younger family members. Or *India*, where elders run the household and often care for their grandchildren. Or *France*, which passed an Elderly Rights Law in 2004 because of so many geriatric suicides and 15,000 people lost in a heat wave whose bodies weren't discovered for weeks. (*ibid*).

My mother can't hear well and she sees men made of smoke. Some resemble flowers. She'll have cataract surgery soon but is too vain to wear eyeglasses.

## A Different Part of Me Speaks

Strip off your skin, put on another. I want a tattoo but it's complicated for Jews. I want an exotic flower, wave, or animal in an exotic spot. My body doesn't behave. It's too late.

I want to be funny, to apologize, to swallow a few stars. I want my recently dead cat back. I want all the hardware of my body and mind to keep on working. If this, then that. You should listen to me. We want a perfect place inside our heads.

I don't have the answers. It's hard to be yourself when you are a large animal in the world. Try another shape. As a child my sister believed in "Lillitoes," toes that spoke and made her cry, asking her to get down on her knees in sorrow. I believe our bodies speak to us, tell us what really hurts.

It would be fun to dance in the air, even if I am asleep. I like going to the abandoned room within me, a dark, rumpled one with a small window, an old bed, a worn desk and chair, unnecessary objects fading in and out. This is where I write.

## You, Too, Can Do This to Yourself

My ex-husband used another name when he was gambling, Jack Glaze. Before I discovered this, I would occasionally call a few poker places in Missoula, Montana and ask if my husband was there. Describing him was his undoing but I needed to see proof. I went to the poker room, inserted myself, stood back, and stared at him. His face turned the color of aspirin. He hissed, "Get out of here. What's the matter with you?"

My first boyfriend's father died, crumpling onto a busy New York street, everyone stepping over him.

## Today

I'm learning the difference between death and life, between a cat's lungs drowning with liquid and champagne in my mouth. I have gathered pieces of a dress I'm trying to sew together, but I have forgotten the order of the steps. Old mountains wheel themselves in front of me, changing the way they look every day, so I won't recognize them. My headaches signify something. I consider replacements for everything because they are so much confetti, ideas I must let go. My dead cat purrs as though I could make him out of anything. There are adjustments.

*Open*, I say to their teeth.

All the ghosts arrive.

## Yesterday

My mother's boyfriend had a face full of sad longing and whitening, curly hair down to his shoulders. I was a teenager and he was much older. He was animatedly, aggressively talking about his new watch, showing me the bright flashing numbers that changed every second as he backed me into a corner of our curtained New York City apartment living room. His body pressed against mine. No one was there that afternoon when he wrapped his arms around me.

Later my new twenty-year-old boyfriend occupied the same redesigned living room. Now Plexiglas boxes, glass, and steel dominated the room. I left my mother and him sitting on a sofa, whose color I can't remember, to fetch a glass of water for her in the kitchen. They were sitting side by side, pillows with modern designs curled into their backs. Their conversation was awkward, stilted, and my mother laughed wholeheartedly at odd moments. When I returned my mother's hand was rubbing my boyfriend's leg.

## Gender Instructions

My heart is not violent.
Dig a hole and fill it with a body of water.
I speak to myself during dance class.
Carve a man's body that spills everywhere.
I was created long ago as a sentence. Bone and skin.
Move your genitals this way, then the other way.
I'm disappearing into a soft body.
I'm still here.

## Yesterday

Can part suffice when the rest is absent? A shadow through light could be my dead cat, encroaching, falling. I watch a friend, who had a stroke, turn something over and over in her bad hand, objects skittering, names hovering, descriptions darting away. A fog suddenly lifts and words are glimpsed as if the brain is playing a game.

## Letter to My Future Self

Dear F. S.,
I imagine being old in an empty room. A large window is occupied with fresh green speckled tree branches. Books are tucked around other books. So many selves are extracted or condensed and sifted into the person that remains.

Place a key and a monocle next to each other on a table. Step back. You see one perspective about what the key opens. People hurt. Maybe it's the key to the just-lit room in which you are old. Put on that silly monocle. Enter. You are a stranger. You peer out the window at a garden where tentative raindrops begin to fall. One eye is blurry. The eye with the monocle sees a blue hydrangea with ashen birds alighting. You like both views, tell yourself two stories that, with enough practice, will sound true.

# Today

As I grow older bones gnarl, muscles form knots. When I speak, it often feels like a monologue. The distance between my skin and brain is shortening. I bleed differently. I could be a broken radio. I could be a television webbed with cracks. I could be a peeling raincoat that spills forth you-name-it.

The first recorded prosthesis was Indian Queen Vishpala, a woman warrior in Rigveda (approximately 3500-1800 B.C.) who lost her leg in a night skirmish called "Khela's Battle." Her fellow fighters fashioned an iron leg so she could continue. (*Institute for Preventive Foot Health, "Prosthetics through the Ages," Patty Boyd*).

- In a Seattle park I watch the face of a child digesting information from a computer tablet. Or is the tablet patiently devouring her?

- I am signaling my refrigerator for more and better food.

- I am ready for new inventions but not the new selves we create for them.

- I have too many opinions; humans as representations of words and ideas that will outlive us.

I've already learned the types of prostheses: hip or knee, arm or leg, tooth or eye, joint or palate, breast or penis. Many of my friends have had replacements. One of my stepfathers had a penile implant. Inside their bodies are artificial hearts and lungs. In 2007 1.7 million people lost a limb in the U.S. (*unpublished paper from John Hopkins and Disabled World*). Cosmesis are prosthetics that look real, with appropriate age spots, freckles, veins, tattoos.

## Tomorrow

Time arrives like a familiar relative wearing that terrible scarf you hate. You don't know what gift or curse it will bring, gratitude, regrets, disappointment. I want to abandon most of my belongings. We are all mundane and miraculous and everything passes.

Some dinosaurs evolved until their enormous bodies outweighed their brains and every gesture became too difficult. Birds shrank and were distilled from other species, reptiles, or flightless, featherless, wingless creatures. Elephants evolved from small aquatic animals. They grew larger, their trunks lengthened, limbs grew longer, and their feet shortened. More than 99.9% of all species that have ever existed have become extinct. (*Conservation of Wildlife Populations, L. Scott Mills*).

## Letter to My Other Future Self

Dear O. F. S.,

I follow you onto a merry-go-round; we talk and I rip up your ghost; I trail clouds, fascinated by their evolving shapes. I can't make anything happen.

It's hard to know when to stop. My head is full of ideas, full of teeth eating everything. Tonight the wind is loud but brings me nothing. I'm older for lost reasons. I look up a little bit later. I don't count years anymore. Point, shake, then pour the rest. I believe in the theory of making yourself clear in the world. But I'm not sure I'm really here.

# Diary, a House

# Outside the Room

Someone sighs, wondering what's going on in the living room, for every room is more than a room. Each room grows hair, ages, its features sag, creating its own particular properties, weightlessness or lathered in raspberry jam, instead of paint, or inescapable like a maze. The inside signals the outside, a warning, an invitation, a reordering or rewarding. The living room tries not to hurt anyone, apologizes and means it, being amicable.

Someone: Why is there a boat in a bottle on a table?
The room: Because my face is washed in light.
Someone: What's really going on in there? I hear high heels going in circles.
The room: People are fragile, with or without their garments.
Someone: Are there naked people in there?
Room: I didn't say that.
Someone: I'm going to the ocean to see my friends. When I return I want them gone.
Room: I'm collecting the evidence.

Someone misconstrues accidents outside, on the streets, knowing how much danger is in the whole wide world. Accidents include unstable cars, epidemics, people behaving inconsistently, alternating addresses, weapons indistinguishable from gifts, language that bludgeons bystanders, a rain of stones, trees toppling, objects in motion, aerodynamic creatures flying where they shouldn't, one thing sliced from another thing.

Outside the house:
the hidden movements of inaccessible animals
the house resembles an angular hat
the moon whispers over the metal shoulders of rockets
the difference between snow and feathers is attitude
people's stories grow from sidewalk cracks
a muscular lake feels the house's breath
the sun decides when it will return
wind says what it needs

There is so much outside the rooms of the house, tentative grass and vegetation and beasts of the fields with their violent inclinations. I prefer beauty, its wildness contained in various ways, in the lithe, moving body of a cat, how objects prefer to be seen, or paintings in museums with primary colors that attract one another.

# Diary, a House

## Bedroom, Jan. 13, 2016

Every room is safe and dangerous. Ghosts squirm into action and wander, reenacting what made them ghosts. Words spoken in an empty room reverberate, returning to the speaker. In Medieval times people had only one space for everything. I, the bedroom, am nestled within a house that is nestled within Seattle, a subtle city. No sun comes through my two windows, only a frozen gray sky, a giant's sigh or a sad exhalation.

Because I am a bedroom there is the usual furniture, a bed, dressers and tables crammed with old cosmetics, jewelry, scribbled papers, pennies, crushed clothes. An animal that appears to be wearing white gloves and slippers is dying. The couple that sleep in the room, a man and a woman, have allowed this creature, with blue eyes, in, close to them, and now must learn to push the animal away. Everything else inside these rooms disintegrates too, but slowly, often imperceptibly, a chair thinning, wall paint streaking and worn, floors coated with dust and dirt, curtains torn, knobs wobbling. They have lived here twenty-six years. The animal can hardly walk and its shallow fast breathing fills a corner, blurting out steadily. The animal is the size of a little plant and dies elsewhere, at the veterinarian. The woman cries. But I want to tell her about unexpected noises, the tapping on floors, knocking on ceilings, the telltale scratching that she will continue to hear. I want to explain about the small ghost in the basement.

## Bathroom, Jan. 24, 2016

Every room becomes a story within a story. The old man with a leg brace that lived here alone before the couple arrived couldn't get out of the bathtub. After flailing, his brace scratched the tub and a neighbor came to help him. I, the bathroom, am a lonely place where people have no available defenses, and what happens is a result of the immediate time and space. They must face everything, and then leave.

In the Roman era, water had religious as well as cleanliness value. In Tudor times people were afraid that dirty water spread illness, especially syphilis. (*BBC, History of the Home, Dr. Lucy Worsley, 4/11/11*).

I am a witness. The woman is a biological room that is often remade, used, left. I have glimpsed sex and hidden fears and secrets. At another house in Montana, the woman's angry ex-husband opened the bathroom door so violently that the doorknob left a fist-sized hole in the wall because their toilet overflowed.

# Living Room, Feb. 2, 2016

Every room is also a door. The woman used to drink and black out when she lived in Missoula, Montana. Sometimes she didn't know where she was when she woke up in the morning. Here, in Seattle, once when her husband wasn't around, she drank wine until she vomited up what resembled red pieces of a heart. She is doing better as she's wearing herself out. Sometimes she's living in the living room. She misses the trees, large and full of photosynthetic secrets, the fresh air, spaciousness, and the circle of snow-embroidered mountains outside. Even though she almost ran into an industrial building in Montana when her car slipped on ice once when she tried to drive home snow-blind.

Before the 19th century, I was known as the "parlor," from the French "parler," to speak. "Living room" was used more widely after 1918, after World War I, during the influenza epidemic, when it was known as "The Death Room" since it was at the front of the house and that was where bodies were held. Before it was a room for receiving guests, and now it's a room for leisure activities that reflect the personality of the designer. (*blogsurabhi.wordpress.com*).

I keep the weather outside. I'm growing older, my expression changing. The man and woman peer out my windows at neighbors, watch television recreationally, calculating how much too much news costs emotionally. Sometimes there is a knock at the front door and someone or something outside comes inside. Sometimes it doesn't open.

# Kitchen, February 21, 2016

People have illusions, wanting to put certain ingredients in a mouth, that certain food is better than other food. They rely on electricity, the way it animates the refrigerator, stove, microwave, and explodes through the house, making everything suddenly alive. I'm a room people feel they should have done better in. What's the difference between the woman's hard-boiled eggs, the man's bones, and rocks? I don't exaggerate. Be careful of my knives and the mixers and shredders that escape from drawers.

The first censuses in England counted only "hearths," a cooking fire over a stone, not the people. Consider times and places, the invention of utensils, graters, food processors. It's not surprising that people ask for more.

# The Yard, March 3, 2016

Neighbors border the lawn and greenery. They come in all varieties. My nearest neighbors have claimed the spaces in front of their house as their private parking spaces. A family lives across the street whose young daughter is afraid of macaroni horses and words made from fire. She sells homemade lemonade in front of her fence in the summer. Sometimes she gives it away for free.

When the woman walked her cat in his harness and lease, she met:

the woman who loves cats, feeding them all, and yet owning none

the grumpy bachelor whose walls are filled with chiming clocks and who owns two flightless, yellow birds

a widow who thinks too much about everyone else's life

the couple who lived on a sailboat for many years and settled into a house only to travel as often as possible

a couple who adore their classic Mustang car, spend all their free time washing it, and believe all the neighbors should be enthralled with its roar too

It's internally and externally satiating to own a piece of land. The sounds of lawnmowers and leaf blowers are the rhythm of something tame that is noisily dying. The children of the couple next door were always smashing a vehicle or motorcycle, and another used to shoot out street lights with a gun and ended up going to prison. At summer occasions firecrackers smile brightly in the sky, bursting with impatience. Some days I go wild, unkempt, with merchandise receipts, candy bags, dandelions littering the too-long grass, chickens clucking from a house a few blocks away. The neighbors are wary, yet friendly, waving at one another, not wanting attention, yet present. All are standing on their property.

# Basement, March 21, 2016

Every room wants to discover something about itself instead of its occupants. I'm the room where bones are excavated. I'm the room full of ghosts, which is about time and its attendant failures, how it is backwards and forwards, inside and out, up and down, sometimes all at once. Time is the enemy, or friend, of the woman and the man, and a part of living creatures. I see the cat that visited the basement often although it no longer resides here. The cat used to jump among the shadows, perhaps for something smaller that moved, insects, mice, rats, a bit of dropped food, or enticing smells. The woman talked to the cat, which a few times tried to say "hello" in return at night from the basement. The cat, too, was searching.

I've settled deeply into hard clay filled with sewer lines, water pipes, and gas lines. During a lengthy rain I leak through one corner and one wall. I'm made of tenacious cement with one wood-paneled room, three crude rooms, and a bathroom, with a shower that once resembled a coffin. There is an art studio, a shop, the man's television room with a speckled linoleum floor and a large room with file cabinets and a washer and dryer. I'm a receptacle for some of the forgotten objects and projects of the humans that live here. I'm still in their dreams.

Sometimes one of three ancient wall telephones rings across from the bathroom as if remembering their uneventful conversations. All are black and Western Electric:

a rectangular one with a rotary dial and a bell-shaped receiver

another more modern phone with a handset, rotary dial, with keys, and a receiver

an old pay phone with a G1 handset, rotary dial, coin return and pull

I'm sinking imperceptibly but the whole house comes with me. I care very little. I believe in slow self-destruction. I believe in being self-contained. Will my ghosts go with me when I am gone?

## Floor, March 26, 2016

What is below my surface but air? Yet I'm needed. Yesterday the woman knocked her blue vase with red flowers off a table, strewing water and red petals. If not for me, people would be walking on air or soil.

I'm burdened with piles of books, a rug or two, their furniture. I see everything. The man collects old electronic equipment, perhaps a symptom for something or some time he misses. So it would be very difficult for the man and woman to move.

During the Middle Ages the floors of peasants consisted of dirt, straw, dung, and waste from the household, compressed by living until it became solid. North American tribes employed sand as flooring and some cultures used peanut and sunflower shells. Egyptians developed stone construction with the pyramids and the Greeks created mosaic flooring. The Romans invented radiant heating systems to warm the floors of wealthy families. Concrete was discovered in Syria at approximately 6500 B.C. and used as flooring. (*about home, "A Complete History of Flooring," Joseph Lewitin, 1/30/17*). This was my history.

I like to spread out. My wooden, concrete, carpeted, linoleum, and tile looks convince the people to keep me. A sprawl of sunlight touches me through the curtains. I enjoy the theatrical placing of furniture and the cat that used to skitter around every object. If I could advertise for a mate, I would claim that I don't exaggerate, and I hope to remain in every relationship for years.

## Closet, April 4, 2016

How do I feel when I'm not yours? The architecture of the human brain turns away. I'm fogged with the dark-haired woman's shirts, shoes, jackets, pants, and skirts. The man sees her underwear, shirts, sweaters, and socks overflowing from my shelves. These stuffed clothes occasionally leap out. My sliding doors are unable to close.

Previously armoires, wardrobes, chiffoniers, or chifforobes were used in my place. (*Articlesbase Closets and Their History, Ron Maier, 5/25/09*). Some types of closets still include coat, broom, linen, utility, pantry, wall, and walk-in. In the 17th century only wealthy people had closets and then the closet was characterized as a small, private room. In Colonial Times the British taxed closets as extra rooms. (*Design the Closet, Christine Appleby, 3/21/14*).

As a child the woman dreamt she was falling from the ornate light in her toy closet onto the bones of other children, piled high by monsters. They held her captive there and the night seemed excessively long. She waited for morning, afraid the world would vanish before she returned.

I am filled and unfilled. Cats sleep inside me on clothes and humans use me. I see their happiness, wrapping their arms around one another. I see their nightmares. I change. Old letters are hidden under the woman's underwear and unused minted coins are secreted under her socks. I want to shout, "Privacy is a normal, unnoticeable name or buying meat without anyone knowing or a large group of people who don't remember you." It's from one of the letters sent to the woman. But the doors insist on silence, especially with the small ghost wandering around the basement.

## Stairway, April 21, 2016

Since her cat's death, the woman has become vague. Everything is blurred and exhausting. She constantly needs her glasses. She doesn't wake well. Her mind wanders across the floors, rests on a window or ceiling, although something is screaming and clawing its way out of her. She is different and she wants all around her to act accordingly. She plucks a jigsaw puzzle, puts it together incorrectly and calls it done. She's always missing.

Count every step, up or down, like a thought. Stairs have existed in some form or another for a very long time, since the ruins of Jericho. My old, carpeted ones greet a closet turned into shelves near a corner that leaks rain. I am narrow, suffocating, and lead from the main floor to the basement. I am convenient. I prophesy unlinearly, seeing what uncoils from a mouth, a pool of red, a former owner fighting with his mother and sister, or a door like a book slapping open, a motorcycle tangled in a fence, a dream filled with jokes, a future where everything is too small. A flurry of feet is my reward, breath settles around me. And then it happens all over again.

# Door, April 28, 2016

What is rattling my knob wants to enter or leave. All these rooms want more future, even if it's bloody or cursed, sad or deliriously happy. I'm a conduit. I have hinges and peepholes and locks. I can do what a room cannot. I lock people in and out. I watch other rooms. I have a trajectory.

My ancestors, the earliest known doors, are from the paintings of the Egyptian tombs. Our shapes include double-leaf, double door, French windows, half door, flush door, sliding glass door ... The oldest doors were made of timber. (*Wikipedia*, "*Door*"). The woman and her sister were kept in their bedroom when they were young and their mother was busy with men. What they wanted was inside the far kitchen refrigerator.

I bray and squeak and moan, gossiping with passersby or with a window. Beyond me could be anything and everything.

# From the Outside

## Room of Worship, the Past

People who are overflowing with dreams want to share them through singing, chanting, vowing, confessing, whatever is leaking from a chest. Arguments ensue. After spiritual consumption the room is left. The objects of reverence have changed over time, once light, cats, birds, cows, or an object fashioned with certain properties, now the focus is on a particular man or woman who might or might not have done something a long time ago. Rituals ensue.

After worship the walls are polished with heartache and longing and feelings meant for one thing that can be transferred to another. How can something so big be contained in the small room? Tradition is an art form. Sacrifices were once strewn among rocks and bones. Now services are more civilized, with few secrets remaining. One life isn't exchanged for another.

Hope crawls across the floor, wishing to be fulfilled. A variety of gods echo in the unseen and sometimes comfort is achieved. Feasts or festivals, and stories or myths form the skeleton of several theologies. In one kind of religion people stand up and tell story after story about their possible injuries or deaths. In another miracles get up, sit in a circle, discuss what they could have done.

## This Room Isn't a Room, the Present

It has a red door that opens to the moon outside, in the distance.
Light from a smudged window walks around inside.
The room is empty.
Calm and silent, there is no traffic, no footsteps.
No one can leave.
The dead visit, a man of smoke, a woman whose head resembles a bouquet of flowers, a cat the color of ash.
They all enter the room. They are the room.
People talk to themselves in the room, complaining or cursing.
The room shrinks or expands.
Listen for breath, rustling like leaves.
Window light breaks anything into pieces.
The room has no name.
Occasionally there is laughter, perhaps from another room.
The room tries on dresses.
At night darkness hugs everything.
The room is reminiscent of childhood.

Empty, emptier, emptiest.
Mistakes peel from the walls.
The room is small and clawed inside.
The room grows feet. It doesn't know how to use them.

## Room without Space and Time, the Future

A man knocks at the door, a parade of people enter.

The hands of a clock on a table wildly spin in circles. Then the clock hurls itself against a wall.

Walls move themselves away, becoming taller, thinner walls.

A table is swept up by a river of light and carried out the narrow door.

One window always looks into dark, endless space punctuated by a few faraway stars and planets.

A person sits in a chair, growing younger in the room.

Neither day nor night appears consistently.

Silence washes through everything and occasionally there's a small sound like water hurrying somewhere.

Sometimes a ceiling or floor disappears, reappearing later in a different material or shape.

The person sits still in the chair, waiting for time, trying to decide how best it to use it when it arrives.

# The Adventures of Small Animals

### The straw man came with me

The straw man came with me wherever I went, although he was a complicated animal, called Cyrus, a companion cat that passed away a few months ago. Another cat, a stray that's an older male, wants us. Sometimes. Some traces and gestures of the new cat are like the beloved cat but it's not the same. There are worlds within worlds (the way my reflection in a mirror must be more real than my actual self, and I don't like my image, which might chase me out of my Seattle bathroom.)

Cyrus was terrified of a cat clock in our kitchen whose tail and eyes moved electrically to and fro. My husband and I used to lift him toward it as a punishment for eating something he shouldn't or scratching where he shouldn't. The other new animal is too large and enjoys flinging himself into the landscape, trying to catch whatever moves. He's too unconstrained to replace my other animal.

Can the body dream without the participation of the mind? As a child my sister had a birthmark like a red tail up her spine. It eventually faded. A friend told me of a woman writer with a splotchy birthmark the color of raw meat on her cheek, near her left ear. Her man punched her on the mark.

In the Wizard of Oz the Straw Man, or scarecrow, needed a brain. He was superstitious about birds and strangling emotions. If a violent wind sifted through him, he would become fodder for horses. Such breath repeats itself, becoming a gesture. His shadow was imprisoned in his straw body. Would I accept a straw version of Cyrus, my former cat?

## The Adventures of Small Animals

1. Before battles with the Egyptians the Persians released cats onto war fields knowing the Egyptians worshipped cats and would surrender without fighting.

2. In Cyprus 9,500 years ago a human and cat skeleton were first discovered in a grave together. (*National Geographic News, "Oldest Known Pet Cat?" John Pickrell, 4/8/04*)

3. In Seattle 1996 cats gathered for a conference about rain, but they scattered and hid when they got wet. (*Me*).

4. In Quanhucun, China cats were domesticated 5,300 years ago because the cats liked the rodents who liked the nearby grain. (*La Nacion, "Gatos fueron domesticados en China hace 5,300 anos," 9/9/14*).

5.　During the Age of Discovery cats rode ships everywhere, floating, eating mice, their eyes shining vividly in the dark.

6.　In Medieval Ypres cats were not needed in springtime to protect the villagers' wool from vermin so people threw cats off of a belfry tower, which is now symbolized by throwing toy cats from high windows and is called "The Cat Parade." (*www.kattenstoet.be*).

7.　Sweden, 1948, the first cat deciphered the language of mice in order to catch more of them. This language was named "Mousian." (*Me*).

8.　In Japan the "Maneki Neko" is the good fortune symbol of a cat, with one paw raised.

9.　Cats in Russia are encouraged to wander through a new house to bring it good luck.

10.　Freyja, Norse goddess of love, fertility, and beauty, rides a chariot drawn by cats. (*Faulkes, Anthony, 1995, "Edda," p. 24*).

11.　Black cats crossing our path will ruin, punish, and/or bring us bad luck (because they remind us of shadows.)

12.　One afternoon my cat dangled by its collar from a branch as a way of arguing about its nine lives.

13.　What was between a familiar and its witch? Flying monkeys had little time between them. The intention was synchronization or travel or moving beyond an event or superstition to understand what really happened.

14.　In Indianapolis, 2020, cats began walking permanently on their two hind legs in order to reach more hidden treats. (*Me*).

## The Surfaces of Ghosts

Being older, I can't trust my body to do what I want it to do. I wear it out, especially in dance classes, remembering what it could do. I'm not sure how much I care about appearances although I still have so much to learn. I'm softer, rounder and, like the Lion, need courage.

My husband makes the best pies, especially the crusts. So how do I arrange words? In a circle? I want to go home, after breaking a foot, after an operation, or often after seeing the doctor. I want to get better with people I know around me. Days that the bone protruded made me tremble so I couldn't move. I would sleep with my foot out yonder, resting over the covers in an orthopedic boot with a tiny sombrero covering my toes. Does everyone have a near death story where they call a loved one? You call them to watch the cat die one last time in its one last life, and, unlike the Tin Man, you already have a heart which might heal. You hope there aren't any more secrets or surprises left for you in this world. You click your shoes together.

## A Disagreeable Imagination

The world is reliable, but I can mistake one thing for another or, for a while, see a very yellow raincoat everywhere. Sometimes gossip, expectations, a trick of the imagination work on me so that anything is possible, the same way the Straw Man, Tin Man, Lion, and Dorothy saw the Wizard in different forms, a beast, a woman, a ball of fire, a giant head, and finally just an ordinary man. The mind is bodiless, the black dress of sky with its various sequins of stars always reaching upwards, towards what the mind thinks it knows. My shoelaces wander, still a toy for my dead cat. There is little left for the living.

## Seeing Inside, from the Present Tense

I'm clicking my heels, but I'm already home inside. Outside, I am lost but searching for love and what could love me. It's a small moving thing. Everything and nothing. Sometimes that thing is writing; I let it out the door in the evening, not sure if it will return. I'm looking for a word or a story to explain what's deep in us and connects us to one another.

Blood and wings, not together.
A bird repeating apologies.
A landscape of decisions, clear horizons.
Dreams unfurling like early vegetables.
The Past crossing a street to greet the Present.
The face of the world covered with beautiful insects.
A piece of glass pulsing like a human organ.
Headlines breaking everything and placing everything gently inside me.

## Oh My God

I used to tell you everything. But I didn't always need words. I wanted to hold onto you to hold onto myself. You used to live in the other Emerald City. I'm still here in Seattle. Nothing has ended. It's just that you're gone.

# Collections of Breath

I want to forgive myself for not having the lion's courage, for sleeping with married men, a circus employee, a high school wrestler, a gambler, a teacher, a union representative, and some of the much older men my mother tried to choose for me because they had money. For not speaking up in writing classes or when someone hurt my sister or when people made fun of me or another person. There were nights I couldn't sleep while thinking about all the replies I should have uttered. I considered all the people I should have been kinder to. I once tried to give an acquaintance a pottery plate my cousin had recently made and just handed me because the woman said she liked it. Even when I try to be kind, I insult someone. I drive my ballet teacher crazy because I give her gifts she doesn't want.

# Listening to Small Animals, a Trial

My mother woke me in the middle of the night as a small girl. She rummaged through my bed at the start of her sleepless night. She repeated, "Nobody loves me." She wanted company, animal love, television. I was suffocated by emotions, tired and then awake. At the end of the night the inquiries began.

Mother: I'll give you a note so you can stay home from school tomorrow.
She hands me a starfish.
Me: No, I want to go.
Mother: Take one of my sleeping pills.
She hands me a porcupine.
Mother: What did your father say about me?
Me: I always think someone is taking something away from me.
Mother: Did you dream about me?
Me: You are always a vampire in a large chair with your back towards me.
Mother: Where is the man I really want?
I hand her a groundhog.
Me: If you listen carefully you can understand the language of anything.
Mother: Where is your father?
Me: Some days I wonder if I already died and didn't know it because I'm living the same life as before.
Mother: I'm stirring my face in the mirror.
Me: As usual.
Mother: I want pieces of everything.
Me: Peel it open. Watch it closely.
Mother: Where are all my visitors?
Me: Birds are attracted to dead branches.

Mother: Are many men coming to see me?
Me: A turtle. A wolf. A snake. A pigeon.
Mother: You could make yourself look so much better.
Me: Would you eat something so friendly?

## A train leaves a gray station

A train leaves a gray station, chases you along the same old tracks. Branches sprout leaves and flowers, white moths, perhaps in the exact same spot as last year. I am attracted to parades and I have a tendency to follow anyone who seems to know what they are doing, a piece of this or that to make their opinions plausible, but it's what I feel that makes me want to burn down whatever I can.

Magic changes everything, unpredictably predictable. The little girl wants to go home and her companions want to improve themselves. Can we stockpile enough belief to create magic? Instead of graying fur I see where the moon has made a wish and left its pale color to retrieve later. Instead of a leash there resides a thin black leather book with stories about religion. Instead of a rabbit is there only a hat? There are tricks we use on ourselves, an astronaut seeing the earth through a window and feeling its closeness, and the tricks we use to convince others, a photograph of the astronaut with a planet poised on his head. Ultimately I want to know what I'm thinking.

## I was lingering over travel brochures

I was lingering over travel brochures, the old stray cat in my lap. I searched his blue eyes for my dead cat's blue eyes. They were different.

People travel in order to lose themselves or find themselves elsewhere.

I was bubbling, boiling, then bursting with the feelings my dead cat claimed. I had nowhere to place them. I was outside, searching for symptoms in our Japanese maple trees and freesia, with their heavy, fulfilling scent. The freesia turned their red, purple, yellow, white backs to me while refocusing on sunlight. I was in a blue plastic chair perched over our winsomely contingent lawn, with its moss, patches of dry, torn grass, and weeds with their own yellow flowers and insistent method of spreading.

The straw man could bleed straw until nothing was left of him, the tin man kept too much inside, the overly large lion was continuously forced to do things he didn't want to do. I had been all of them. I wouldn't get better if I went home. I needed a receptacle for my effervescent emotions. The wreckage of me wanted more than a myth or story to carry in my mouth.

Writing, and perhaps traveling, was a way of placing those little things, the details of a radiant life, somewhere safe, out of harm. Yet it would soon be postponed for something else of interest around the corner, another book or image or thought.  I would not forget.

## Travelogue to Nowhere

The highway through Seattle, north to south, is clogged with travelers hoping for somewhere better. They have multiplied the same way popular girls do.  I was auditioning obstacles, a mountain that can climb you, a barren interior landscape, a lake so close you have to take its photograph, large rocks squeezed around each other.  My husband and I never had children although sometimes the world told us to.  We were both ambivalent.  Some people might say that's why I fit myself emotionally into my cat.  Or it was my mother and my mostly-absent father's oddities.  But couldn't they say that about my husband or whomever I loved?  Aren't we all tourists?

I hear too much whispering and I dissolve, although I no longer care much about being liked.  But I am discussing places, not people, and the verbiage of going from one spot to another.  I can only occur in one location at a time.

I'm living in a city of people asking them to portion themselves, one after another.  I have cloud-like gray hair, little makeup, comfortable clothes.  One person watches birds unraveling from the sky filled with taller and taller buildings, another is lathered in their job, another is a cog in their dramatic family.  We have all chosen water, ghostly mountains, ceremonial clouds, the snorting sound of rain.  Some of us have cats and others don't.

Because we can see the mountains we like to visit them and the forests and the handful of beaches that surround the city.  Ducks, geese, turtles, beaver, and herons glide on the available water but cats are notoriously bad travelers.  Cats are bound to their territory while dogs go where their pack goes.  When I was a child, our family had a small black poodle named Beauty.  My sister carries the dog's ashes with her wherever she goes.  I have placed Cyrus's ashes over our mantle place.  A photograph of him dangles from the urn's throat.  Months later, he's still everywhere.

Everything goes on.  Spring this year began cloudy and cool.  All those spaces that had been empty were filling up, expanding with exuberant grass, new shaggy green leaves, fiercely colored flowers fringed with puffs of disagreeable tiny flying insects, and spreading blossoms, shaped like hard candy with twists of petals on their ends. Now it is sunnier, growing hot, 84 degrees, in April.  My cat liked sun, 72 degrees, like me.  All is fully blooming around me.

When I see photographs of Cyrus, the same feelings are invoked deep in my chest although I know I can't touch him.  I shuffle through travel brochures with anticipation and curiosity, not love.  The truth is that I'm also happy when

I forget everything, especially that he's gone, and I expect to see him. He was familiar and personal while traveling is the opposite, impersonally there (although I can narrow my interests) and the thing about going to a new country is that it's so different than anything I have known, new language, culture, landmarks. Perhaps it will jar me out of my old life. Visiting a foreign country is imagining or borrowing another way to live.

I blunder through. Although there are travel writers who recommend where to eat, what to see, where to go, in great detail. I like their certainty. I can pour myself into my writing. I can be anyone, anywhere, live other lives, discover my own. Our minds are ripe for our imaginations. I carry paper and a pen everywhere. Occasionally I reread something I have written long ago and forgotten, and sometimes I don't like it. Often I do like it.

In the past I have mostly traveled with my mother and/or sister. The experience hasn't always enhanced me. I remember highlights or vast problems from trips, destinations not reached, carrying my problems along with me. As for specificity, time and place, I can't remember much unless it was famous or unless I recorded it with a photograph, in which case I had a memento and could immediately forget it. As I grow older, much of my memory fades or melds. It's hard to remember when you have two days here and two days there. Yet I'm strangely attempting to make new memories by imagining new situations with my dead cat.

When I travel somewhere I can become anyone, as in books, songs, or movies, where characters are transformed by their desires and interactions. I try to wrap some of the cities I visit around me, doing what I like, seeing museums, literary hotspots, or unusual architecture. I follow the moon over water, scrape white-hatted mountains. I soothe the ashes of my dead cat. There is light and air, food, and a house and a husband.

## On the Verge of

We believe we will find what we are looking for elsewhere. Tired of our lives, scrawled together, tired of just getting by, we are waiting for someone to say they care and mean it. Can a ravaged place be the one for you? Will the perfect place want any part of you? While we are searching, we find ideas or actions that replace other ideas or actions.

My mother travels when she's bored. At almost ninety she's been to China, New Zealand, Africa, Russia, Australia, Scandinavia, Iceland, most of Europe, Mexico, and much of the United States. She likes gambling and cruises. I like to stay somewhere a little longer to see if some part of a new country will seep into me, stain me.

The place for me will be a city of exaggerations, where everything is too large or too small. There could be a lesser god there. Every home is provoked by a sizeable yard and sufficient sunlight. Seasons are simply symptoms. A man, preferably my husband, will be living there. I can peel a potato and still remember its eyes. Story after story involves a rambunctious pet. I will be allowed to move anytime I want. Nothing will enter me unless I allow it. I'd be content getting to know another mind. Romance sustains the unloved and I want to hear all of anyone's lunatic ideas. Wherever I'm going I hope the people there will forgive me.

## Postcards:

## Seattle Strolling

Dear Sky,

I'm drinking coffee, which cuts my words in half. I have done what I've been told but, so far, it's a waste of time. I'm walking from my street towards the water which is coming to greet me, rimmed by mountains with shoulders covered by white shawls.

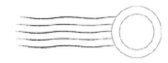

## Tahitian Sky

Dear Cloud,

I'm unfolding and refolding myself to try to force myself out of grief and back into love. I am stubborn, remembering places, events, reliving moments through cell phone photographs, memory and reenacting what happened once like postcards sent from a faraway island.

I remember how Cyrus trembled when an airplane passed overhead. Sometimes the plane tried to write something in the sky that didn't last.

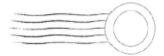

## Postcard from Home

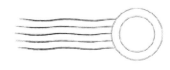

Dear Poet,

Everyone says these things will pass.
Which means: please, quickly. The Seattle skyline has changed rapidly in the
last few years, reaching upward like
someone trying to grasp more air. I open
a window onto my street in Ballard,
which has hardly changed. But then I
live, mostly, inside my local head.

## African Reincarnation

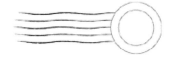

Dear Today,

I would take my cat home even if he
returned to me as a fish, a bird, a straw:
man, or a dog. It began in the shelter
when he first turned his blue eyes toward
me and swatted my hand since he'd just
had surgery where I almost touched him.
I want to visit a place where animals
recover.

## British Sightseeing

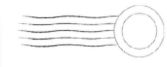

Dear Ocean,

My brick home glistens with rain. I can accommodate myself to your smile, your speech about lies and houses and life without certain modern necessities. I need a bucket to shovel small talk away. Sometimes my future seems all wet.

## Eastern Washington Digging

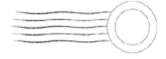

Dear Past,

My good friend made a vase from an animal skull he discovered near the Cascade Mountains. He said he heard it speaking to him. I cried. I listened.

## Anywhere but Here

Dear Containment,

My home is a box of memories; walls, windows, doors, a bridge between a labyrinth that isn't safe, a location to write and decide, a receptacle for shadows and light. Come visit me.

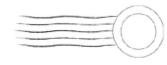

## Greetings from Seattle

Dear Rain,

My body moves here and there, although it appears to be the same, familiar. My body will interpret my mind and go where my head wants. I have expectations at home that I would not have elsewhere.

Anyplace but here is nowhere I want to go.

I want to start again.

X

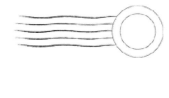

# Part II

# Ghost Notes

# I Was One of My Memories

# I Was One of My Memories

The animal and I breathed on one another in our sleep, our exhalations meeting at some invisible center. He adjusted his head to his best advantage. Yes, he was appealing, his fur a soft nest raked by my fingers. I rested my face on his cushioned ribs, soft pillow that he was. He smelled slightly sour like the last century. A paw stretched then covered his blue eyes. Back then I knew what to do with myself. And I knew time as a human process that continued tangling itself biologically. The animal, my elderly cat Cyrus, died several months ago and my longing is slowly growing smaller.

On television every day I watch strangers dying on the roads of foreign countries like abandoned machinery. All surfaces have become impossible and fraught with meaning. I play back the animal's gestures, his eyes meeting mine, his utterances, on my devices. I have a box of his found whiskers and I still see him everywhere he used to be.

I concentrate on one detail at a time, a white paw with a black spot, his blue eyes fragmented, looking as though his iris had been dropped and shattered. He was watching me, the cracks in his eyes from age. I recall his movements, how he desperately wanted to catch a crow, which would hop away or fly at his approach, or a squirrel. But one time he ran behind a squirrel that was turned away from him, eating something, and he gingerly sniffed the squirrel's tail, then walked away.

I, too, have wanted: an ant farm, but I finally let all the ants loose; a stuffed beagle, with big eyes, droopy ears, and a sprouting tongue like a rose petal that quickly fell apart; a gold necklace that turned out not to be real gold.

# Flutter of One Dream inside Another

The gods would move closer, if they could. I let blind, sprouting scarlet Japanese maple leaves stick to my face like dried snakeskin. Geraniums, purple and red rhododendrons, wisteria and lilac petals bloom everywhere, draping everything. My fingers are small and thin in the earth. I walk where I want, remembering how I needed to run home to you, how I hope to see you now in a different form, a streak of white with black in a field, behind trees that appear unhinged from green grass. They make me tremble. I am kind to the others, the old stray cat, the friendly neighborhood animals, volleying birds, although they aren't you. A staggering pale moth makes me look toward it hopefully still. Even though I know he has gone, the way all of us eventually will, dragging our beastly wants. Occasionally a rabbit will save me, a brief glimpse and a bewildered contentment rises inside me.

The world is different, setting itself on fire for no apparent reason. It's a season and all species have them. New growth is built upon the old. Humans thrive amid frayed or gone trees and vanishing animals. The surfaces change. What will the earth do when it is done with us? Bump around space telegraphing its needs until they are met? It's a body after all. I want to say that since he is gone, everything appropriately slides through my fingers while I'm deciding what to become.

## Surplus Soliloquy

What is it that initiated everything breaking open with color? The soil under my feet is squeezed, sifted, and sung to by worms. The bleating rain arrives, followed by startling sunlight with its slow warmth. The busy sky and ground gather and empty both enormous and microscopic animals that spread richness and seeds. A landscape is created.

I could fall apart at any time, my right eye throbs, my back aches with its strained and sore ligaments and muscles, but the world grows routinely beautiful. Sometime later the world, too, will disintegrate, in its usual seasonal times. We're both cyclical.

## A Brief List of My Ingredients:

I am citied but miss rural sights and settings.
Machines can make me forget everyone, temporarily.
My family's voices contain abandonment.
Stones are my friends.
My cat once stumbled through my pastels and emerged blue and red.
Flies inform me about glass and the illusion of escape.
Too much stays inside my face. A cat listens.
My friend disassembles and studies a skull as if it's a clock.
My sister rains, surrendering.
My mother is a machine gun unavailable for further comment.
Clouds smile when they expect less from the sky. Clouds dream about lost balloons.
I am developing muscles to be used like curtains. I am atomic yet visible.
An old stray cat kneads my hair as if I'm his mother. I am no one's mother.
I am unsure what I need to say with words.
Talk wanders, puddling in my house.
Seeds are warnings about the future.
Something sad is happening.

## What If I'm the Only One Not Taken?

The electricity in my house goes out, soon turns back on again, exploding through the walls and appliances. A disturbing wind sweeps through the city, and the sky is filled with pets and acquaintances, who don't like me anymore. They are floating.

My doorbell rings and something outside the curtained windows is gleaming too much. It's night, and I want to lick the floor, call for my husband or sister or someone else I know.

They are gone, and a dim light enters the barricaded and locked house through cracks and keyholes and door thresholds. My dinner sandwich haunts my mouth, suddenly tasting bad. I don't understand how to stay in one place.

I want to discuss this. Everything nearby is shrinking. I want to say that I do have an intergalactic mind, but nothing escapes my mouth.

## The Myths:

1. *Cabbit*, Japan. A cross between a cat and a rabbit, which is genetically impossible.

2. *Cactus Cat*, Southwest America. At night a bobcat with a long spine and armored tail that slices open cacti, drinking the fermented juice and screaming until morning.

3. *Chimera*, Greece. A female lion composed of a goat's body and a dragon or snake's tail. Seeing a chimera heralded disaster.

4. *Hombre Gato*, Argentina. A human/feline male that scours rural areas at night for animals and people.

5. *Maniticore*, Persia. The body of a red lion, a human head with shark's teeth, bat wings, a loud trumpeting voice, and a scorpion tail. It leaps far, repels magic, speaks as a human, and eats its prey whole, leaving nothing behind.

6. *Matagot*, France. A spirit in the form of a black cat, which, given the first bite of food at meals, will produce a gold coin the next day.

7. *Mater Cattus Horribulus*, America. A female cat/human hybrid, with sharp teeth and claws, that destroys its own offspring.

8. *Neman Lion*, Greece. A lion whose gold fur is impenetrable and whose claws slice through everything. Killed by Heracles.

9. *Sea-Lion*, Phillipines. A lion with webbed feet and a fish tail, who fought terrible storms and won.

10. *Wampus Cat*, Oklahoma. A woman cloaked as a mountain cat who spied on the men in her tribe. The medicine man punished her by making her half woman, half cat. She still roams the woods.

11. *Yule Cat*, Iceland. A large, mean cat that eats people who don't work hard enough to earn new clothes and offer them to the cat by Christmas Eve.

## A Bird Hovers. I Think It is Something Else

Everything is not what it seems. One thing is masquerading as another, a caterpillar as a moth, a fleshy seed as a twitching flower. Small things grow big then shrink again. All that rose's redness isn't held inside. My cat had once comforted me, knew me well. I had done the same for him. I am scraping together and reforming what is left into someone I want to be.

## Radiant Wreckage

My god can hide in greenery, fur, or skin.
My full name is waiting for me. I am dressed in ribbons.
Time disappears and is found inside.
I wear friends around my neck.
I build another self-portrait out of leaves.
My bones are sticks.
My new lyrical earrings aren't enough.
I tediously swallow someone.
I stop wobbling and conveniently choose a side.
I am out of character as myself.
My heart petitions for small things.

## Life-Sized

I witness rain with small syllables. Everything tiny demands attention. All those miniature experiences, objects, living creatures, build our lives, make them larger. It's a slow process that seems too short in the end, the stunning flower, the ghostly curtain of snow.

I will exert myself across the surface of events until I find what I'm missing, that weightlessness like fingers lifting my hair or water falling excitedly from a great height toward more water, robust companionship, the extension of my purposes.

## Ghosts and Mirrors

Are we a transitory species or its conclusion? We are always looking for something better. Once three or four other human species lived here concurrently. We aren't the only ones to have resided here. (*Smithsonian online, "What Does it Mean to be Human?"*) The DNA of all varieties of human beings is 99.9% exactly the same. Every cell in our bodies date back to the emergence and evolution of humans in Africa six million years ago. We nearly became extinct 50,000 years ago, decimated to 10,000 adults, until we adapted. (*Smithsonian online, "One Species, Living Worldwide"*)

The past ignites the present and can't be changed. Ghosts are synonyms for the past. The smell of other animals and a penchant for answers is the present. The future is someone just out of reach who could be right about everything.

## Recipe for Fur

(Makes two servings)

6 familiar animals
2 tails (or substitute 8 ears) in another bowl
One large cylinder of whiskers
½ cup insinuations softening

Stir the ingredients, then slowly add the mysterious ones. Mix well.
Add color.
Add animal opinions.
Pour into two clear pans and bake for ten minutes in an oven. Remove and let cool. Pat your skin with everything remaining.

## This Didn't Happen

I was talking to myself in a room of books in order to understand another person. There was nothing about a mirror in this action, nothing to hide, although everything that happened later had a story about me. Does the form that evokes this vary? Would the story grow more complicated?

How I would love to have what I once had, the exact duplicate of the unfolding plant resurrecting itself seasonally. There are so many variations and influences, windows that don't open or close in a room, sky simmering with stars at the front door, a bed twisted grotesquely, nothing more written on the walls of the room brimming over with books.

Move the room to hovering over a sea or gliding toward an ancient castle no one knows.

## Still Life with Other People and Animals

What can be rescued from the world is a who. We live in intervals, people, or cats, returning to tell me something, offering or taking something. One of my memories was of reshaping myself to my childhood, when I dressed as a blood-sucking woman at Halloween, just before my father was banished to a nearby hotel by my unfaithful mother. They both liked to exercise themselves on others, most of the time they forgot my sister and me. I learned to live closely with animals, evolving around each other. The first witness was Beauty, a tiny black poodle. Later I knew I was missing obvious attributes. But because my cat was gentle I left my head in his small mouth.

# I Am an Animal

# 1) I Am an Animal

I'm beginning to mewl. I miss my animal parts, portions that instinctively know what to do, what's needed to survive, that push through the world without fanfare. I am part of a larger world and a tiny piece of the natural world. I lost my elderly cat several months ago so it might be a way of keeping him close.

As an animal I don't have to buy anything, attend a job, speak or even whisper, nurture my dreams, drive a car, fix the television or radio, read a book, see a movie, work on my personal fulfillment.

Animal:
I pry what happened before from what happens next.
Borders and countries are changes in light.
I presume nothing has a happy ending.
Something is dangling from a cloud's mouth.
Earth understandably shifts away from its memories.
Where are you standing? What are you doing?
I listen to what the distant stars are saying.
I slip through objects filling the empty sky.
Wind carries all the necessary information.
I lose myself in bones and smaller animals.
Air is broken yet smiling at a piece of meat.
I keep the moon and sun in sight.
There is you, me, this.

When I lived in Missoula, Montana, from a distance I saw a grizzly bear heaving itself through the mountains, an elk stilled by noise, deer that crept into a yard or halted in open fields. In and outside of Seattle, where I live now, I've seen a hawk pondering its anticipated direction along my backyard fence, green-splashed hummingbirds pausing mid-air to evaluate me or my cat, waddling possums, greedy raccoons, an owl turning to stare like a wrist twisted suddenly.

Who can live without language?

Human:
Words can be stones, gestures, certain breathing, expressions.
When instructed to annihilate an apple I find several methods.
I use a variety of pronouns.
Actions cannot accommodate me.
Phrases about the human body are comic.
I write my name everywhere.
Like animals or funhouse mirrors, we don't do what we're told.
I try not to lie but you don't have to believe me.

The body uses ears, eyes, mouth, limbs, and fur.
I wasn't always like this.


My cat that recently died used to cry "Hello" from our basement when he was lonely in the middle of the night. I personally prefer murmuring.

Although I struggle to comprehend the here and now, I, like any animal, love and hate, preferably without thought. I enjoy water, food, a safe place to sleep, a robust fire with a good burn, or its equivalent. I hurt, am jealous, forgiving and unforgiving, funny, sad, joyful, cruel, mysterious. I wander toward a surprise, from which I'm never sure I'll return.


This could be me:

1. South Korea. A gene was inserted into a beagle so that under ultraviolet lights the dog glowed. (*New Scientist, "Fluorescent puppy is world's first transgenic dog," Ewen Callaway, 4/23/09*).

2. Soviet Union. A "multi-dog" was fashioned by transplanting a puppy's head and front legs onto the neck of another dog. The creation survived for six days. (*Wikipedia, "Vladimir Demikhov"*).

3. Massachusetts. An unhearing human ear structure was grown on a mouse. (*Mother Jones, "The 8 Weirdest Mice in Research Labs," Sarah Zhang, 8/22/12*).

4. California. Scientists are attempting to grow human replacement organs inside pigs by designing a human-pig embryo. (*The Guardian, "Scientists attempting to harvest human organs in pigs create human-pig embryo," N. Davis and K. Rawlinson, 6/6/16*).

5. Germany. A scientist wanted to prove a human brain was attached to "wires," to the nervous system. He filled a kitten's cavities with zinc and silver and the kitten died within twenty minutes. (*List Verse, "Most Bizarre Animal Experiments in History," Mark V., 10/30/13*)

6. Oklahoma. Researchers gave an elephant a high dose of LSD, after which the elephant moved in erratic circles and then died. (*List Verse, ibid*).

7. Virgin Islands. A researcher's female assistant lived in a water-filled house with a male dolphin in order to teach the animal to speak English. But when the young dolphin became amorous, she reluctantly masturbated him to put him at ease. (*The Daily Telegraph, "The woman who lived in sin with a dolphin," Florence Waters, 5/30/14*).

8. Virginia. Nearly three thousand baby jellyfish were launched into space to test the effects of gravity and had vertigo on their return. (*Popular Science,* "*Space-born Jellyfish Hate Life on Earth,*" *Shaunacy Ferro, 10/15/13*).

9. Massachusetts. Duncan McDougall weighed humans before and after their deaths and the patients had lost twenty-one grams. He killed fifteen dogs replicating the same experiment. Finding that the dogs didn't lose any weight, he concluded that dogs have no souls. (*Historic Mysteries,* "*The 21 Grams Theory,*" *Jim H., 1/27/10*).

## 2) Not in this World

The disappearance of birds leaves the morning unsung. I'm unable to lose myself in lyrical agreement with sky. There would be no hummingbird visitations or pigeons or gulls or grackle sightings. No eerie owls haunt what moves at night. I'm not finally awakened by a cat that prefers avocados and corn. A lack of insects, those undersized specks with legs, antennae hopping or flying, stinging or transporting pollen from place to place. No historical coats or food or domestic pets gathered and living beside us. No flowers or fish erupting from waves or quiet water. No reptiles, amphibians, birds, mammals, insects, mollusks, crustaceans, corals, arachnids, or worms.

At the Seattle zoo the meerkats scurried and froze in their exhibit, a swarm with one lookout for impending danger. When I'd taken a sketching class there, a keeper allowed us behind the scenes, where I heard their surprising constant chattering through their overhead wire fencing. We also visited the inside cage door of the tigers and one young male had stretched himself over the door frame as if he wanted to crash against us, his claws spread. Everyone else was terrified by the gesture.

The snakes were all tongues and rough skin behind glass. I was attracted to drawing the flamingoes whose bright pink/orange feathered bodies contracted and expanded in the open-air exhibit with its stagnant water, swooping sky, scattered trees that hid the newly born. The penguins were sleek and graceful, mere dashes of black and white, underwater, awkward on their rocks. Coyotes and wolves glimpsed our group from behind bushes and clusters of trees. Gorillas positioned their burlap bags, hung between trees for relaxation or wrapped around them, protecting them from onlookers. The hyenas paced. The elephants wearily moved their bodies from one spot to another, considering everything with their trunks. Hippos resembled surfacing rocks underwater and lumps of gray coal on land.

In Montana a mouse lived somewhere behind my sink, raiding the bread drawer often. Its parade of tiny grain-shaped shit and the partially eaten plastic bags with fists of bread were more than clues. The invisible mouse had outwitted my cat, who might have dropped it inside initially weeks ago. I removed the bread. I locked the drawer. Still the ghost mouse shouted its existence, concentrating on that particular drawer as if the bread would miraculously return. I set a trap and the mouse ate the bread without springing the device. I bought a better trap that resembled a tongue and the clever mouse navigated the release, stole the bit of cheese. I imagined the mouse laughing at me. One morning I found the dead sad little fur body with perky ears, long thin tail and tiny scrabbling feet on its side, in the mechanism. I threw the body in the garbage. It had become a game. One of us had lost.

## 3) The Body Continues

I have lost half of my thyroid, an ovary and my fallopian tube, as well as a number of cysts that shouldn't have been where they were. Cats, a parent, and numerous things I have misplaced are forever gone. I'm unfolding in the creation of my own story on the other side of a door that opens and closes of its own accord.

I have scars and I like them as pale, slender reminders of memories the way animals lick themselves, cleaning over and over. A spider twists away from me along a wall. All our lives are short, unplanned skirmishes. I'm more fragile as I grow older and parts hurt for small reasons. Floaters and flashes appear in my eyes, my skin grows thinner. Soon people's names will be dust in my brain. A dog's head turns away from me, towards its owner. We both look at the man calling the dog to him, not certain the dog will follow.

## 4) A Shrunken World

There is nothing more to prove; a tail, claws, the territorial breath of rain, nocturnal observations, the inability to do as much as I used to. My mind wanders. Everything becomes a suggestion.

I have a friend who cries when she takes writing workshops. I think everyone should cry more, especially in writing classes. I laugh when I'm nervous, deflecting.

I need to disperse myself more, other than reading, writing, ballet, synagogue, and attending some of Seattle's cultural events. I need to pollinate. Isn't that what people do when they shrivel, become hard little fists? Human body cells replace themselves every seven to ten years. Snakes shed their skin periodically, outgrowing them and rub hard surfaces so their skin often comes off in one piece, which shocks people finding the discarded skins. Cats molt their winter fur coats for lighter summer ones. Dog coats are sensitive to the length of sunlight. Hermit crabs outgrow their carapace, bury themselves, then eat their exoskeleton. Birds replace their feathers between one and three times a year. Nearly all insects go through metamorphoses from larvae to winged adults in stages. (*Wikipedia, "Metamorphosis"*)

I try to pay attention to the signs around me, darkness arriving late, a whistle in the distance, a hummingbird curiously reading my face. Our bodies contain our sentiments, our ideas. I know I can only be the beast of myself.

## 5) Everywhere Else

In today's Seattle Times (*"Your head on a new body," Didi K. Tatlow, from NY Times, 6/11/16*) I read that a doctor in China might begin human head transplants soon. My mother has claimed other names, other nationalities, a different hair color, religion and age. She has stated to men that she doesn't have any children and that a number of people are jealous of her.

I:
borrow my dead cat's blue, blue eyes.
crawl into my books.
see where sleep and being awake lead me.
jettison my body slowly for another.
don't do what I've been told.
sweep away old memories for new ones.
arrive somewhere I've never seen with all my pieces intact.

My afternoon shifts, moving to another spot, circling round and round until it is comfortable. Caring for my animal is such a simple action, a matter of empathy.

I have had one animal save me from another:
my first beloved cat screeched at my ex-husband when he was yelling at me.
a strange threatening dog on my walking path was chased away by a larger dog.
a snake near me, in some brush, seemed deterred, frozen, by the specter of a hawk.
an annoying, overzealous fly was soon glued in a spider's web from which I didn't extricate it.

I am a conglomeration of all the animals I have known, even briefly, and loved.

I could be:
a fish with words bubbling from its lips.
a parrot that can only speak about water.

huddled deer trying to cross a busy street.
a sheep with its provocative face.
the cow stumbling toward grass.
a horse pensively leaning over a fence.
a young alligator squeaking its name.
a dog with brown patches and soft fur.
a turtle drying himself on a plastic island with its plastic green palm tree.
my dead cat whose shadow neatly folds itself into a heap at my feet.

List of questions:

who is the fly caught in unnecessary chemicals
will something happen
can inventions lie
does a story believe itself if no one is listening
who will go away and who will arrive
will more experiences with allegories occur
when will day invite me inside the blue bakery of its sky
should I look
should I leave now
is this the end or the other end

# Momentary Confessions

## 1) No Stranger

My obsessions propel and focus me: the hardness and longevity of rocks and minerals; transitory handbags and shoes; landscapes designed for animals or events, but not both; animals with stories that speak to me with gestures; books filling up my windowsills and tables; how writing accumulates within me and then bursts; ballet and how parts of the body can rise toward the sky; art and layering paint; and water with its embrace.

The past ignites the present. Most deaths eviscerate what is collected in a heart but suffuse everything. As Tolstoy said on the subject of happy families, every unhappy death is particular in its own way. My cat died several months ago. I still want to apologize, although he didn't suffer much, and I wasn't responsible.

Obsessions are repetitive, and no matter how much I try to suppress mine, they surface like flames in a burning house. They lead toward contentment, happiness, perhaps even ecstasy, at least for a while. Swallowed, they escape a mouth again and again.

Four people are eating dinner in a house whose windows are smeared with dead insects. There are two couples. The men work together in a shoe factory attaching laces. One man rummages through his wife and children's dressers and satchels when they aren't home for clues about their lives. The other man recalls an old girlfriend's kiss years ago while watching a movie. One woman unbuttons her shirt in a bedroom and holds her breasts to a mirror. Another woman stares through a window at the landscape, with its woven tree branches and patient sky. Which of these people are compulsive?

Other peoples' obsessions include: plaids, stamps, coins, toasters, pens and pencils, soaps, Barbies, nails or other metal, Hello Kitty, sports, news, weather, sex, telephones, bandages, polka dots, Christmas ornaments, biting, wealth, cats, dreams, memory, illusion, betrayal, and other people they know or people that are famous.

## 2) Momentary Confessions

Some choices are personal. Collections are often about objects, and I have accumulated my extracted teeth, books brimming with unusual language and messages, rocks (especially tourmaline, agate, and amethyst), shiny jewelry, tiny cat figurines, colorful old plastic radios, and secondhand clothes. People enjoy the things that will outlast them, satisfied in knowing that they are in their proper places. Some people go further, consuming them, intentionally destroying them or acquiring them and abandoning them. Do we reflect something larger, something embedded in our society, country, bodies, or the world? My husband owns so many books he doesn't know where a specific book is located. We stumble through his knee-high piles. He owns tools and old electronic equipment with dusty and rusted metal gears, stiff tubes, fraying wires, plastic knobs, and calibrated machine faces. Is older really better and more interesting? These objects can have disturbed histories.

## 3) Not Good for Much Else

The various degrees of compulsion determine the possession. There is admiration and joy in perceiving the object and owning it, and there is often the need for absorption to make the object part of ourselves. I have collected a box of my dead cat's whiskers, fur in a locket, and ashes on my mantelpiece. A girlfriend, who is a visual artist, spends much of her time viewing other people's artwork and she buys what she can. In America we are what we acquire, a house, a car, a plantation, land, art, domestic pets, children with pigtails, being a capitalist society in which we are encouraged to purchase more. *Risk* is a board game whose objective is to militarily obtain all the territories on earth. *Imperial* is a German board game for anyone over twelve years old to win the wealth of all the available nations.

What is the difference between need and love in our cravings? In *Lolita* by Vladimir Nabokov, Humbert Humbert (an obsessive name) begins, "Lolita, light of my life, fire of my loins. My sin, my soul. Lo-lee-ta: the tip of the tongue taking a trip of three steps down the palate to tap, at three, on the teeth. Lo. Lee. Ta." (*First page of the book*). H.H. is a man clearly obsessed; "my only grudge against nature was that I could not turn my Lolita inside out and apply voracious lips to her young matrix, her unknown heart, her nacreous liver, the sea-grapes of her lungs, her comely twin kidneys." (*p. 165, Second Vintage International Edition paperback, 1997*). "My heart was a hysterical unreliable organ." (*p. 258*). The definition for the noun of love is 1) an intense feeling of deep affection 2) a person or thing that one loves. (*Google*).

Collectables:
clocks staring attentively
the absence of bones in a woman unzipping her skirt
a tall heavy man with a clipboard approaching on a beach
a sky bubbling over a foreign country
an ornate teardrop earring, a cigar box, splashes of red ants
the discovery of parrot-colored butterflies
coral illuminated like language
missing parts of the world you just left
counting and recounting all the tiny spoons from every state

## 4) Unreliable Possessions

I berate myself over details. An obsession can take me out further from myself and my problems. I forget all else and focus on the desired action or object. I am inside a cavern yet I can see something shiny and apocryphal outside. I want to make it mine. Some objects can transfer their power to us, or so we believe. Our obsessions change over the years just as we transform and grow. My ex-husband regularly gambled, using another name, and did drugs. When does recreation tip over into compulsion? After death, nothing can be collected except by others.

Collecting contains the acts of discovery, acquiring, labelling, filing, exhibiting, and storing. This preoccupation can manifest because of a fear of shortages or losing something valuable. It could be related to the hunting and gathering instincts embedded in human history, although animals, too, hoard food, particularly rodents and birds. Some human collections include back scratchers, belly button lint, cell phones, hammers, and miniature chairs.

Other Collections:

>hours of unreasonable explanations
>superfluous superstitions
>demented dating conventions
>cracks in a body from icy cold
>teacups painted with circus scenes
>jars of animals with wings and claws
>evenings with a moon made from feathers
>tails in a box of guns and knives

## 5) Imaginary Collections

1. John F. from Indiana, knows how to count to ten in Italian, has a girlfriend who has a pet macaw called Misunderstanding, is a salesman of medical equipment and collects affection in glass jars.

2. Susan G. from Portland, sleeps on an ancient, patched waterbed, is recently divorced, wears button up trousers, is an eye doctor's assistant and collects canine teeth in black velvet bags.

3. Andrew N. from Toronto, goes everywhere on a bicycle, eats too many Chinese cookies for their fortunes, is single, works at a fast food restaurant and collects prosthetics just in case he might need one someday.

4. Taylor W. from Seattle, eats only meat, just broke up with another girlfriend, works at a metal tube factory and collects stuffed walruses.

5. Freckled Gustav S. lives in San Francisco, with his mother, is secretly in

love with his dentist, likes seminars on personal crises, is between acting jobs, used to collect memories in enormous albums but now collects sex objects and toys.

6.  Belinda H. in Philadelphia, is married with three children, likes to read books about hands and fingers, sings a favorite song to herself before she falls asleep, wants to learn the rhumba and collects melancholy in napkins.

7.  Michael T. residing in Tampa, tried to hug an alligator as a baby and has scars on his arms and chest, says he's married to his boat, wrestles reptiles as a living, has memorized several poems which he mutters to himself as he collects thunder in baby bonnets for his cat.

8.  Peter G. lives in Arizona, often wears a suit, is searching for his brother who disappeared as a three year old, never has had a close relationship, gives guided tours of ghosts in Phoenix and collects irrelevance in plastic quart bags.

## 6) Museums of Obsessions

Alaska: the Hammer Museum, our species' first tool.

Arizona: the Museum of Miniatures, all things small.

California: the International Banana Museum, 20,000 items related to bananas.

Connecticut: the Trash Museum, with a history and artist mural.

Florida: Coral Castle Museum, a man spent 28 years carving the castle with home-made tools.

Idaho: Oasis Bordello Museum, situated in a brothel that was active through 1988.

Illinois: Busy Beaver Button Museum, buttons and more buttons.

Indiana: the Museum of Oddities, hosted by Indiana Joe in Metamora, Indiana.

Iowa: Matchstick Marvels, models and sculptures made from matchsticks.

Kentucky: Vent Haven Museum, ventriloquists and their dummies.

Louisiana: voodoo and bloodletting at the New Orleans Pharmacy Museum.

Maine: Umbrella Cover Museum, the loveliness in necessity.

Massachusetts: the Museum of Bad Art.

Michigan: Moist Towelette Museum.

Minnesota: because the Spam Museum is rebuilding, the House of Balls is still open.

Nebraska: National Museum of Roller Skating.

Nevada: Erotic Heritage Museum.

New Jersey: Silver Ball Museum, arcade and pinball games.

New York: Morbid Anatomy Museum, beauty and death exhibits, history, and ideas.

Ohio: Wyandot popcorn Museum, collection of poppers and peanut roasters.

Oregon: Vacuum Cleaner Museum.

South Carolina: Kazoo Museum.

Texas: National Museum of Funeral History.

Utah: World Puppetry Museum.

Washington: Dialysis Museum.

Washington DC: the Museum of Unnatural History.

(All the above from Yahoo Travel, "51 Weird Museums Across the U.S," 2/4/15)

## 7) Hungry for the Lesson

A voice inside my head criticizes me. It's a dark chambered unit muttering about lost opportunities, stale thoughts, the unzipping of the unnecessary. Whose voice is it? My mother's, my god's, my cat's, mine? I burn letters and photographs and then they must be replaced by their equivalents. That is when obsessions are born. I have abandoned some, my crammed rocks and minerals, my art created from acrylics, puzzle pieces, ribbons, chalk, and other assorted materials.

I still miss my cat, scouring all signs and space for the memorable bits of him. But mainly I return to my reading of experimental and overlooked writers, being one of them.

I'm trying not to save things, knowing, since my cat's death, that I can't save anyone or anything, including myself. (Imagine obsessives saving the world like strange superheroes). All those objects can insulate someone from experiences. I try to inhabit the minds of others. I'm grateful to my imagination, which can take me almost anywhere, even though I personally remain understaffed and my eyes become faulty as I age.

We are all fighting nothingness with something. Loving something beyond its material worth is considered obsessive, from whimsical to deeply disturbing. Compulsions fill us with specifics, staving off personal oblivion. Is it enough to know our revered objects are somewhere in the world without us?

# Mistaking One Thing for Another

## Mistaking One Thing for Another

My life is placid. My fictional characters and animals are another story. I'm in a house of ghosts, watching, describing, orchestrating. Imagination whisks me away yet positions me somewhere deep inside in a space I didn't realize was there. The house could have ornate furnishings yet no electricity or running water, the locked windows could be painted with perpetually relaxing lush green and blooming summer scenes, but no air enters the rooms. Shoes have to be removed and socked feet spring from parquet floors, the bathroom within a maze and hard to find. A writing room with a window containing a plum tree and assorted bushes is next to a room filled with devices for torture. The bedroom is full of nooks and crannies and the shadowy silhouette of a man is painted inside a closet door. A piano in the living room seems to play itself. A real plant with deep green oval leaves climbs the cabinets in the kitchen and threatens to overrun all the older appliances. A large city park spreads out from the front door, but I've never been outside, have I?

My past visits me as I wait for something to happen. My dead cat, Cyrus, comes and uses my feet and heart as pillows, certain I still belong to him. I lift a thick novel from a nearby pile of books, holding it in both my fists towards my face. The more I ignore him, the more he wants my attention.

## Undisturbed House

I am recreating myself. I need another house to hold me, one that is sleekly mid-century modern, one that can ignore the past and concentrate on the future. I will situate it in the soft, natural gestures of the country. This house heaves itself up high, using rectangular structures. Indoors my breath slips from nearly empty room to room as if it had begun to slide and there was nothing in the way to stop it. This allows me to imagine being everywhere in the house at once.

## Reinventing the Body

Some people are infected with tattoos or piercings. Some have animal whiskers implanted in their cheeks. My mother has had her face lifted, her nose redone twice, and goes monthly to remove her wrinkles, to be less of who she is becoming. Yet her face falls again, her nose shifts as she ages, and what will happen if she stops her monthly treatments? We express ourselves through our bodies. In the meticulous mirror, we want to see reflected who we could be.

## Time Holds Out an Imaginary Hand

Early on, everything was animated:

insolent dolls walked, cried, shouted their names
animals were part of the family
falling water formed words or sentences
toy trains bumped violently
small metal trucks scooted from one room into another
clouds with names were your friends
cracks in sidewalks were avoided to stave off broken backs
balls and balloons flew through the air, never landing
plants knew what you were thinking and acted accordingly

Fairly recently there have been investigations inside the brain, fumbling with belief, information, and recollection in the thalamus and neocortex. Possible experiments include: one place, too many pieces; sorting action figures into groups; pushing slow bones, or other objects, around in a circle; finding unreliable footnotes; inserting colors where they aren't usually found; and naming a city that hasn't been reached yet.

In the 1960s and 1970s, cognitive theories, drugs, visions, and dreams emerged, such as a life lived as a yellow lamp or clouds drifting across your shoes as you are walking or a dreamer surrounded by weeping tear-shaped dinner plates and food dangling from the sky's mouth or thirst like smoke storming through a body or stars rotating too quickly like someone fumbling with their keys.

The future is:
a sky clogged without rain
ghosts coming and going, carrying stones into small, palimpsestic cities
poetry as a carousel of words
towns haunted by boys falling from clouds
lonely things pressed against the mouths inside our bodies
the implication of the world is that something outside our bodies remains

## Still Life with Invisible World

I was in a figure group for many years where we unpeopled our models. Often the models wore only hairdos and socks. Occasionally we draped them in clothes or costumes or offered them props. Summers we convened in someone's backyard edged with high, articulated bamboo so neighbors wouldn't be surprised by a naked model. Although everyone in the group saw the same thing, the image was sifted through our various experiences and each of us painted or drew radically differently. Some created realistically, others interpreted the body as another form of landscape, and others unpackaged the scene so it appeared stripped to its essential lines, or there was a Cubist or more Impressionistic vision, with many layers and colors. I have created versions of Cyrus, tailless and tailed, in Sumi inks, self-portraits with elemental questions, pleasurable flowers and plants, landscapes with juxtaposed scenarios. Some paintings explained how I felt about ballet and one was donated to a dance group auction. I went with another group to sketch restless animals at the Seattle zoo. An artist is someone who sees the less that is there.

## Inconsequential Injuries

I am composed of:
    twig-bones and carried by the nape of a thin neck
    the graying of my birdcage haircut intrudes
    brown eyes that detect flurries of encroaching dark, torn pieces of paper
    (floaters) and darting light (flashes)
    my features stretched onto my long face
    a ghost cat develops holes as he rests on my shoulders

I live in an expensive city possessed by rain and sometimes I fail when I speak, language bunched up within me. My husband is trained to take care of problems as the variations of my personality go out for walks. My shyness often doesn't know what is meant while a new disorder holds me together until I get there.

## How I Live Now

I'm decorative, engaged, whimsical, and advertise myself with my companions. I try to adapt to changing circumstances the way a favorite chair feels when you give it to someone else and then see it again. I extract and eat all the chocolate chips out of chocolate chip ice cream. I'm left alone often. When my cat died, I wanted to drink excessively but didn't. I am manipulated by domestic animals, but I hope my husband doesn't learn how to do that. Now I pet everything I can. I ask too many questions. I abbreviate my past and elongate my future. I'm often on the verge of sleep. I'm neither bored nor happy nor sad. Everything matters, but I can explain nothing. I borrow other people's minds so I can forget my own. I'm tired of routines and yet they, and the ghosts, sustain me. I've amassed too many illusions. New desires can ruin me like fire, with constant disagreements. My intention is redemption or, minimally, reupholstery.

## Brain Boxes

*Female*:
Something is sparkling and shiny like jewelry!
What did they mean by that?

A piece of gossip melts in my mouth.
I listen. I understand. I pause for emotions.
*Male*:
Tools and more tools!
Something good to eat that won't be noticed.
She was mathematically wrong about everything.
I don't know how I feel about that.

*Cat*:
Something is moving!
I'm not sure about what you said so I'll clean myself.
Sleep is refractory and nearly as appealing as food.
My people need me so I will remind their tall legs.

*Autistic Son of a Neighbor*:
My DVDs!
I play them and play them.
My body is bitten by words and touch.
My hands rush away in the air.
Why doesn't anyone hear what I'm saying?

*Mother*:
I have plans.
My children have other plans.

*A Sister*:
 I'm waiting for money and kindness!
My sister and I have developed unfinished holes, tunnels.
Why can't parents realize how betrayable we are?
That too-difficult love isn't enough.
The chore of being alone is simply a symptom.

# Accidental

Cyrus and I are in a boat, and I'm rowing while watching him curled contentedly on a bench. We are circling and circling on calm water, going nowhere and fine with that. We are "in the moment" although there is no such moment in real time. I already know what my daydream is telling me about myself in relation to remembered words and deeds. What it is I enjoy, actually love. My dead cat is now a myth that other cats are compared to, like a new boyfriend in relation to all those before him. Company? Yes, and my childless method to care for myself. I want to discover the secret to the life-long magic trick that I watch over and over again.

Imagination is surprise. It tolerates and encompasses. Imagination holds hands with reality but slips away. Imagination recalls all you've said and done, even if you have forgotten or have tried to forget. I have hidden myself from my elderly mother who would use me against myself. She requires that I call her every day. She expounds on the details of her ordinary life, where she went shopping, what she bought or ate, which part of her body itches or aches, her men, her parties. She doesn't like it when I insert myself. But the person I've hidden asserts herself anyway, to other people, in dreams, in writing or dance. This other person needs to live her life.

There are spaces reserved for a happy family, an affectionate cat, writing, art, and a neat house. No one needs to leave or die, although imagination can have its own fabricated events. One of my mother's boyfriends dared me to steal a ring in Marrakesh. I did it for the dare. The act didn't seem real, but I didn't dream it.

## A Collection of Mistakes

For periods of time, in dreams, thoughts, or writing, my mind forgets my body. I'm jolted back into my life by lifting a coffee cup, restlessly rising, ambivalently speaking. Splotches of light leap across walls, distracting me, releasing me from my current reveries and plunging me into others. Have I forgotten that young girl with her sister closed in a dark bedroom, told by their mother not to leave until her new man had left? We were told not to exist. But apparently the girl hasn't forgotten me, especially in the way I desire but I'm afraid of attention, or how I dislike darkness.

As a writer I like to create shorthanded scenes, where chairs have emotions about being moved closer to someone they don't like, a homeless person speaks to a ribbon of beach every day, or weather studies astronomy. My mistakes perch on my shoulders, commenting on my actions. Who hasn't learned from burning their fingers on a scalding cup? I tried a lot of drugs and liquor to find the ones I like. My house contains a variety of histories, within its structure and the objects it contains.

That bargain meat wasn't a bargain.

The old stray cat that likes us watches television as if it could help him understand people. Animals outside us become familiar with our weaknesses, which inspire their own. When the old stray turns toward me his face is half-light and half-shadow, one side empty and the other focused on me. I'm not sure whether he is asking for something, perhaps permission or reassurance, or comparing me to what's on television. My body dissolves in darkness and I can't find anything. Perhaps it's simply flickering light or moving figures the cat notices.   The kind of light that illuminates one thing and then another.

# A Cure for Secrets

# A Cure for Secrets

My young mother wore an old-fashioned long gown that crept across the wooden floor behind her as she walked. Six-year-old-I was crammed into her bustle, step for step. We sashayed across the floor at the television studio. The audience and attendant personalities needed to guess what my mother's secret was. I could barely breathe. I was a girl sewn back, close to her mother. We undraped, pulling, uncovering one another after fooling the onlookers. When was a girl like a dress? I liked the clapping, the surprised looks. We won seventy five dollars and roller skates. The CBS show was called "I've Got a Secret." I still do.

Inside each secret are instructions about pain and pleasure, the things that don't want to be reconciled or said out loud. Secrets love their beginnings and their discovery can change how you view something, someone, or an action, while an obsession generally doesn't change or transform what surrounds you. Both can be internalized. A secret can manipulate or hiding it can be a manipulation. It is usually tucked away while an obsession is overtly repeatable.

Some of my secrets include:

pretending to be asleep at night to my cat or husband

disassociating when I'm bored although I appear alert

my childhood companion, a pillow named Suckalee that I licked

talking to myself (once my ballet teacher said, "I can hear you," which meant it wasn't a secret anymore)

liking too little rather than too much

My mother spent at least sixty years lying about her age. My sister didn't speak about some of the things our father did until he had died. My husband's and my quirks are complementary. My husband forgets to tell me things. When I'm quiet, he speaks and vice versa. He cooks aimlessly, without recipes, and I eat his spicy eggs and vegetables. If he drops onto one knee I sit on it. We are sanguine, choleric, melancholic, and phlegmatic but at different times. Sometimes I pretend to be an animal, usually a cat.

Animals have secrets, maps of personal danger, puzzles involving food, storage, or forgiveness. Sometimes they run into the street after something illusionary. They swerve from other animals, reading hints in their gestures, poses, facial expressions. Submissive animals are directed what to do. Hidden sexual preferences can make or break a human being, a density shattered like planets, bodies poised in various positions at once.

We assume that if someone isn't forthcoming about what they did that they're harboring what they are ashamed of, which may or may not be true. I give my secrets away sparingly to friends, as I want to share slowly and get to know them better. Every so often I choose the wrong secret, and my friend is disgusted, like the time I told a girlfriend about picking my nose as a child and studiously placing snot in the hair of a troll, which I handed to a visitor to admire. We compare indiscretions, my past drinking to a girlfriend's cigarettes. I decide to whom I want to impart what particular piece of information, my sexual history or foibles with my husband, my impatience and propensity to do things immediately with my nervous friends, my boredom and predilection toward trying new forms and subjects to other writers. I'm a house with rooms filled with oddities that don't know about one another because the doors are closed. I invite select strangers inside.

Shame is a rare commodity these days. Some things are integral parts of my personality: something fermenting that wasn't meant to; what was inside out or held in my mouth too long; a scared, stubborn cat; pinching my newly born sister whose young flesh didn't deserve it; a body primitively slipping into another; a locked room filled with festering confessions.

Animal secrets:
butterflies feel colors
a snake sculpts a long stone with its skin
parrots like hideous furniture and are afraid they are irrelevant
fish consider their sex and its antonyms, depending on the environment or hormones (*livescience.com, "10 Amazing Things You Didn't Know about Animals,"* Ben Mauk and R.R. Britt, *3/30/16*)
salamanders remake lost organs or limbs (*livescience.com, "Missing Parts?"* Tanya Lewis, *5/20/13*)
certain jellyfish (turritopsis dohrnii) renew themselves again and again, becoming immortal by reverting to a polyp stage at will (*Wikipedia, "Turritopsis dohrnii"*)
cats are not jealous because birds migrate
owls prefer a dreamless sleep
dogs dedicate their personalities to their owners and savor stink
peacocks enjoy domestic celebrations

## I Have Been Seen in My Underpants

Growing up in New York City I have learned everything I need to know by peering out my family's apartment windows. I have seen: sex, from its dainty or wounded beginning to its postscript; fights, using gestures, silent words, or objects, blood splattered on glass; young children bouncing on ruined furniture; people reading in bed, at a desk, on a toilet; people dancing to unheard music alone; skeletal people ballooning and large people shrinking; a dog stealing food from a party plate; a man working at an office naked very late at night. In that reluctant city every act before a lit, open window at night could be seen and during the day people forgot or didn't care as they put their gatherable selves together. It was a perverse treasure hunt.

As a child I liked to look out my window on nights I couldn't sleep to see what other illuminated windows would keep me company at strange hours. Now I'm alert to the ghost of my dead cat, hearing him in the house, as if there isn't much else going on in the world. His ghost is an echo, a concealment being whispered or a reflection on a windowpane. There is always an inside and outside to everything.

In Montana there wasn't visual comradery with strangers because of all the open spaces. But once, when my car slid off an icy road, all four cars that passed me stopped to help. In Missoula, in a house outside the town, with its circling snow-clamoring mountains, I would sometimes wear underpants and an undershirt while watering my garden, on a road where no one could see me.

In Seattle, just past downtown, in an area called Pioneer Square, there are three blocks where, after the Great Fire of 1889 the city was built on top of itself. The two levels coexisted with different businesses, the more furtive below, until 1907 when the bubonic plague arrived, and, because of the numerous rats below, the underground was sealed off like a terrible wound. If Seattle was a person, he would never come to a decision about himself. A polite, unrevelatory man who grew larger, sharper, more modern, becoming younger as time passed just as the odd surplus and small one-owner shops transformed into glass and steel behemoths. Seattle would be the kind of person who revised the worn, the historical, with something ferociously and optimistically new. He didn't need to speak to anyone for days, grew tired of cars, was pleased with the constant murmur of electronics, wanted to be taken seriously, gazed at carpets of water, was accountable for the remaining flimsy forests, often shook the vast ambitious machinery of rain loose, didn't know what to do with those hands, and could occasionally stray from long-held opinions.

Apartments and townhouses are beginning to fit inside each other neatly, yet a personal privacy still prevails. After many years, I know things about my neighbors. An unprecedented number of serial killers originated in this area. I live on a street of houses and my neighbors have gathered and tended their private lives while doing yardwork, falling over themselves or their work, or hauling away a likeable desk or dottery chair. They are much like me, staring at a tree, sitting alone in the grass, waiting for a plucky breeze or a narration (preferably from rain).

Secrets are their own destinations, carried within. Tourists aren't invited. I have seen my overweight neighbor's underpants when she bends over her beloved car, and I never want to see that again.

Secrets are foreign bones, radio forecasts (spirits swarming from the woods), and over time, resemble snow (white asterisks that advise air).

Secrets unbound: breathe out (a whirring noise) and leave with sad abandon, join in a parade with boys hoisting tubas, leaving their little shoes at the door, never reaching the vagrant sky, hold fists of coins in an exploding house, and apologize for what is self-inflicted and getting around to making us better than we were.

## The World Can Be a Destination

Embarrassment used to be a form of social control telling us how to eat overlarge meat, the biography of a bad lawn, what to say to a nameless child, what to do in case of an indecent accident. Those times are done.

My horoscope suggests that I should be kinder or complete my sentences.

## The Secret Life of Secrets

Secrets are busy clenching someone's heart, consulting a nacreous moon, sprawling inside nightmares, replacing what you want with what you'll get. They turn away from what is there and keep you awake at night. Their dreams are a theoretical childhood or what you are missing or something so deep and dark you can't recognize it. I speak to the mouse in my kitchen drawer that's no longer there because it seems visceral, stealthy, and suddenly dangerous. I say, "Go away." But there is no response and I know that the mouse can't leave because it's already gone.

## A Short Guide to Confession

My mother, who prefers not to be Jewish, has been to a church and confessed a handful of her sins to a priest and said she felt better afterwards. She was relieved. I am a rucksack of odds and ends, inadvertent bones, who doesn't get much from confessing to others, but I do murmur and contemplate to myself and wonder why I didn't say or do something else. I am wrong often. But to speak anonymously is what I have done much of my life, in my family, and it isn't helpful. I take a deep breath and consult myself. I try to change for the better although I do see the attraction of speaking your episodes out loud and then handing them off elsewhere like naughty children banished to tents outdoors where you no longer need to claim them. They are separate, diminished.

I dissolve slowly with friends. I confess everything to my husband, even before he was my husband, but occasionally there are surprises. I want to be a person who eases into her surprises.

# Accommodations in a Lost City

# Accommodations in a Lost City

Every summer raccoons climb our plum tree and shake and shake it until something falls. Every winter intermittent rain arrives in Seattle making everything slick and malleable. The world is spinning and can't help itself. Even further away galaxies, made of space and time and matter, were formed and are still forming because of forces applied to objects.

Persistence can be beating your head against a wall and it can be outlasting everything else that has quit. I do both. I have had unrequited interests, including Paul McCartney and Benedict Cumberbatch, the practice of ballet for several years, which I began in my fifties, and writing, which sometimes feels like a stone dropped into my hand. I have a friend who insists on a relationship with a woman who keeps trying to forget him. Perhaps he will become the one suitor who will pass all the tests in a fairytale to win the princess.

Dali depicted the persistence of memory in a painting, melting clocks in an empty landscape with a distant figure of a man. This is how we are plagued with time and space and Dali implies that there is more desolation to come like the persistence of relentless aging. My old stray cat, my cat that died, and other animals continue in their usual activities, running, catching, playing until they can't do so anymore. An apple jettisons itself from a tree, birds veer, migrating toward what they believe they know, fish swim longingly for something they can barely remember. The world turns and turns every day, sacrificing a bit more of itself. We lose something too, time, respect, money, as we try to accomplish something more.

We borrow and insist as we live flesh and blood lives. My sister rocked back and forth on her knees as a child before she went to sleep, hitting her head against the headboard, while I stubbornly lure language to take some of my shape, half woman, half words, a kind of mermaid. I'm better among sentences, but must live on land, so I roll my eyes toward the sky, having relinquished my first husband so I could find and marry my second one. I've always hoped, in defiance of the facts that my mother would learn to love me.

Because of supply and demand, my once lost city, Seattle, punctuated by water, is currently enlivened but it has its moods. Aloof, inaccurate, and formerly a repertoire of gestures, it now is reinvigorated, fulfilling, accurate, and still moist. The city persists in its changed form, but it has sacrificed comradery and a relaxed notion of itself for self-interest and expansion. There are growing pains. A mermaid finally abandons her fish legs and can walk on land but is no longer special, charming, or fanciful. She misses her water.

The architecture of the body holds its own little city: children of various ages stand in front of a rose garden; all those afternoons of absences and confidences; an assortment of superstitions.

My grief is a shadow not a mirror.

My habits hover, meet in secret, and then make demands, boxes of minerals and rocks, fractal maps, bird feathers, dangerous books, narrative art.

These houses unravel limbs, release another wandering heart.

## Assaulted with Gravity

An obsession is conspicuous in its accumulation of objects but persistence isn't as overtly noticeable. It hides in ideas, thoughts, preferences. It hides in mountains disappointed by sky or water sternly pursuing water. Persistence lingers. It sometimes gets sidetracked going from the highway to a road or street to street. But it's traveling somewhere, has a destination, even a theoretical one, like avoiding an illness or insisting on a cure. My ninety year old mother wants to persevere until one hundred. As a teenager my sister thought about killing herself and I, the older sister, convinced her that she would have a forthcoming, chosen life. A friend of mine's sister did kill herself, leaving a space that could contain anything.

## Fragile Occurrences

Twenty seven years ago my mother and sister came to Seattle for my second wedding when I was thirty six years old. Beneath the rim of blue sky and torso-shaped clouds, our ferry chugged to Bainbridge Island for a visit and then back to the city skyline. This was the day before the ceremony. On the way back to Seattle, my mother said she was having a heart attack. I called a ferry worker over, who began dialing 911. My mother said she was feeling better and not to call emergency services to helicopter her off the ferry. My sister and I tucked her into her hotel bed and soothed her, taking turns. She moaned that it was okay if she died soon since she had done everything she wanted to already. My mother will be turning ninety soon and I'm the one who feels I'm running out of time.

Left unsatisfied needs persist. I'm a footnote in an enlarging city. Many people go to Hawaii in the winter months, attuning themselves to the warm weather, tropical foliage, coffee, breathing underwater, sugarcane, the ragged linearity of cliffs. I had gone to Kauai with my first husband on our honeymoon, and we golfed there, but the marriage only lasted three years. We drove, circling the island several times, sky repeating itself wherever we looked. We saw a pig roasting underground, impossible flowers circling people's necks, a reenactment of native dances that explained their history, the balance of nature through movements of hands, feet, and hips. We watched the ebb and flow of the beach through our hotel sliding glass doors as the pool seemed to fit itself closer to our lanai. Palm trees displayed coconuts, undulated, studied us as we studied them. Sometimes we walked backwards on narrow paths through the lush forests or along the bluffs in order to see a view, a flower, a plant, a bird. That husband and I both remarried. He died a number of years ago of a heart attack at the natural food grocery store where he worked.

## Rabbit Parable

Persistence is a rabbit that lives in a suburb. She wants to have a party tomorrow for the other animals who live nearby, two possums, several raccoons, frogs, rats, and a clever coyote. She has invited the dogs and cats that live in the houses, but they're not sure whether they can attend. Insects and spiders have their own parties. And birds, especially small ones like hummingbirds, say they will see which way the wind is blowing. The rabbit enjoys her incessant requesting and hasn't thought what to do about the party at all.

"Is it your birthday?" a green snake inquires near a shopping mall. "Because this sun is so bright a cake would melt outside, and the cars are blinding."

The rabbit doesn't want to tell the snake that she just likes to ask.

"Hey, I heard there's a chicken wandering around a Big Chick parking lot. Let's go see."

The rabbit and snake infest the drive-ins and parking lots of all the fast food restaurants looking for the elusive chicken.

"I love routines and useless gestures." The rabbit twirls on her hind legs because the cement is fragrant with meaty juices and odors.

The women that walk by smell of oranges, lemons, make-up, perfume, lavender, and oatmeal for their skin. The men smell of steaks and swimming pools and the scents of the women. The children chase the rabbit or throw hula-hoops or raise their cell phones to take a photograph of the wild.

"I don't think I belong here," the rabbit confides to the snake.

"All the more reason for a party," is the reply before his body stiffens into a strange posture and he hurries after a querulous squirrel.

"We can't help who we are," the little rabbit murmurs at the window of the pet store to some fish circling and circling, their fluid conversations inside a bowl.

"Yes we can." A fish curves around its own emptiness. "We are all failed creatures, but we can keep trying." The fish moves its mouth so bubbles rise to the surface and pop. "My search is endless," it says, swimming around the same corners again and again.

The rabbit hops to a large supermarket where a small dog runs out with something red and dripping in its mouth. "There used to be hunters and huts and wild animals roaming this land years ago," the dog barks after gnawing the meat and swallowing it. The dog's owner hurries out and chides the dog about its future. "Who do you want to be?" she yells.

At the Chinese restaurant the rabbit is invited inside. There is a benevolent red and gold glow to all the furniture.

"No package food here," the owner states. "Good place for party," as if he is reading the rabbit's mind.

The man nudges some chopsticks toward the rabbit and brings a sampling of salty, sweet, sour, and spicy food and sets it on a round table. The rabbit briefly tastes everything and smiles. She relaxes, leaning back in her chair, as if the very thing she has been looking for all this time had been found. Oh, she had tried to have this party for so long. All the animals, dogs, snake, rats, cats, squirrels, frogs, possums, raccoons, coyote, and even the wandering chicken, show up at the same moment as if they had already received invitations. They fill the restaurant suddenly, eat all the remaining food, and then they leave. The rabbit is left nothing but the bill, which the man says she must work the rest of her life at the restaurant to pay.

## Marital Predictions

My second husband has flourished. In the twenty seven years we've been together he has become more nervous, attentive, grateful. Sometimes I know what he'll say before he says it. He can't predict what I will say, which is fine. He once tried to leave me at his parent's house, when I didn't know them yet, so he could take a trip with his twin brother. We hardly take trips together. The desire for sex endures. While he doesn't like yard work, I do. He cooks preemptively, drives more, and lives in a house more cluttered than the one I want to live in. We will shrink into one another. We don't have children, so silence will follow us, although our lips are constantly moving. We fit together in most ways. When we have a fight, which is seldom, I stop talking to him until he can surpass his stubbornness to glimpse my way of thinking. I have made him cry, which broke my heart. We both suffered when our elderly cat died. My husband is patient and I am not. He has long toenails so he won't get ingrown ones. He likes old things, including me. I am five years older than he is. With all things machinery, he needs to be right. We play good cop/bad cop in many different situations and I'm always the bad cop. We both work part-time, often together, and use our own faces for what's to come.

We found Seattle separately and met through friends. He arrived at my rented house with its disjointed rooms for our first few dates. I wasn't very interested, having recently divorced and what was broken felt continuously in danger of breaking again. I was a ghost exercising her possibilities. I was a mermaid trying to make a living. He had never been married, had a mustache and thick black shoes. I had my suspicions but eventually abandoned them. Our mouths staggered and he grew tenacious about marriage. I declined and declined. He removed whatever was stuck in my hair, brushed it. I said yes. My throat stopped its drinking. The city ached from small earthquakes, weak houses, tender boats, and water gathered everywhere. He decided NO a week before the ceremony. My breath betrayed me. We both did better, married. We were lucky, collapsed into one another. For twenty seven years we've spoken what we knew, found a phosphorescent gentleness, squandered our bodies, and sought proof for our revisions, living in the same city where we started. It could have happened differently. And I'm still asking, *Are you coming with me?*

# Familiar Phantoms

# Familiar Phantoms

When I was young my mother claimed to have an enormous stick ready under her bed if my sister or I woke her up too early. One day I actually searched for it but didn't find anything. I wondered if she kept it in a safe, secret place during the day, reviving it at night. Or perhaps someone had borrowed it for their unruly children. My mother and I seemed made of different stuff altogether. I didn't understand her. She sometimes threatened to send me or my sister elsewhere, boarding school, to an unknown or imaginary relative, out on the street to play. I was afraid of her. I still am.

My elderly stray cat, that found my husband and myself, is scared of everything, any small flamboyances like an object not in its place, a visitor, a hat, children, squandered gestures, a ringing doorbell on television, wind moving branches, rain, pennies in jars, a body's sudden movement, a sneeze, a sigh, a laugh. He is curious but often afraid. Yet he is comfortable with animals and odd noises in the dark, chasing things from the sky and earth in the black of night. He is wary of quick, unfamiliar things or things that throw themselves at him. His tail goes down and he runs as far as he can. I'm afraid of other things, including certain everyday objects and gestures that aren't what they seem, obscuring their intentions, as well as heights, a clown, a doll, a mother's or a friend's kiss, a kitchen knife, and some of the people I know. I understand their capacity for harmful behavior.

The lion in "The Wizard of Oz" believes he is cowardly and unsure, yet he acts bravely when threatened. He relies on the Wizard's drink to make him become someone else. I, too, became a different person when I was drinking, looser, more seductive, more defined and sure of myself. I thought I drove more confidently. Most of this wasn't true but it was what I believed.

Fight, flight, or freeze.

When things or people don't act in predictable ways, the result is either fear or fun. Many years ago I was hesitant to confess to my ex-husband one morning that the toilet in our rented house was overflowing (he banged the bathroom door open so hard the knob created a tiny crater in the opposing wall). I was meanly gleeful when three young male Mormon missionaries found their way to our isolated Montana home and my ex-husband, who smoked a tremendous amount of dope, waited behind the front door (he yelled curses at them and they scurried away, abandoning their usual discourse). Mostly I was fearful of the person he was becoming as his restaurant business, money, and friends were failing or leaving. A resignation grew on his shoulders that had leaked in from the rest of the world. Yet he did know how to have fun and recited some questionable, extremely funny jokes that I no longer remember (I'm terrible with jokes). Personality can be slippery. And what can make me laugh can also make me cry, depending on context.

Common fears include small spaces, failure, intimacy, migrating spiders or snakes, clumps of cockroaches, people, heights, encompassing water, endless tunnels or bridges, needles, being rejected, flying, driving, difficult tests, public speaking, the dark, evil such as ghosts, demons, and monsters. (*The Washington Post,* "*America's top fears*" *Christopher Ingraham, 10/30/14*). Many people I know are afraid of being alone, abandoned, or poor.

These are possible body responses to perceived danger: stomach problems (dyspepsia), tightening of blood vessels (pooling), increased heart rate (tachycardia), accelerated breathing (hyperventilation), muscle tension, "goose bumps" or rising hair follicles (piloerection which causes animals to appear larger and ready to fight), focused hearing, sweating, increasing blood glucose (hyperglycemia), and sleep disturbances. These changes help our consciousness define the emotion of fear. (*Wikipedia,* "*Fear*").

The amygdala in the brain processes emotions, secretes hormones, and decides which memories are retained. Without it, fear disorders occur or fear is disrupted, for instance, a mouse will approach a cat. (*biology.about.com,* "*Amygdala,*" *R. Bailey, 4/15/16*).

When certain birds, reptiles, fish, insects, or mammals are threatened, they emit "alarm pheromones" to defend themselves and let others of their species know about the danger. Detecting a stressed rat's odor will cause other rats to flee. (*ScienceNews, Scicurious,* "*The scent of a worry,*" *B. Brookshire, 12/23/14*).

The other night my husband rose from his sleep and wandered around the house. The cat continued sleeping on my legs in the darkness and neither of us moved or made any noise. When I finally asked my husband what he was doing, he said that he was searching for the cat.

## Primordial Reflections

Fears are part of human nature and have helped species survive and evolve by learning what to avoid. For me this includes heights, my mother, my ex-husband, who has died, public speaking, and potential car accidents. My self takes on a life of my own. My relationship to my self is a long butchered process and can only take me so far. My selves are strung ornaments, bewildered and watching for what might happen next. This is why communities, and eventually cities, have formed, so we can avoid or escape whatever could occur. This is what we have persuaded ourselves to believe, even after we have killed or imprisoned everything that once could have killed us.

An uncertain future influences our morality, frightening us into trying to be good, as in the consequences of drunk driving or trying to do something constructive with our hands. A fear of God can be seen as a passionate mouthpiece for the unpackaging and repackaging of the self, or it could be something deeper, swelling, but not necessarily contagious. It also leads to political and cultural manipulations, the fear of immigrants or poor people or terrorists or other countries, and it stains our election rhetorics, in order to influence our vote or teach us how to quiver under our school desks in the case of an impending atomic bomb.

A child's classmate makes disturbing faces at school; the child joins in.
The opposite of flowers.
Someone eliminated from a photograph or painting.
Whisper a war story to a baby.
I punish myself for mistakes, then fear myself.
I'm absent everywhere I look.
A woman leaves a red message on a mirror. She vows to always use birth control.
At a horror movie the woman likes to study everyone's panic.

## Unseen Negotiations

1. On a foreign mountain, 1944, the man was exhausted by the melody of bullets. Clouds shrugged, his left eye rained some liquid, stars were beginning to take the shapes of the dead men whose names he knew, so he called the clouds by new names. His tongue was dry, his left arm broken in two places. A shadow behind a rock reminded him of his patient cat. He remembered unrepentant trees bending over him and a woman, a two-headed lamb, a box of his mother's talismans, a bird smitten with him that he nursed back to health at his house. He saw something shiny and small in the tall grass of another country. As he bent, reaching for it, a man stretched forward, grumbled a gun toward his face. The startled man shot the frightened man, who was about his own age. The man unrolled the dead man, wondering what kind of music he once listened to, whether he had traveled much, if he liked children. The man knew he could easily have been the dead man, but he accepted the medal for bravery when he returned home.

2. My father was king of the stones. He told stories about grabbing some curious cow's tongue and pulling, or clouds clinging fearfully to burgeoning trees when they spied his face, or how, way back when, everyone was your enemy if you were the king of something. My father mussed my difficult hair, pinched my moss-afflicted arm until I felt

inadequate. I dreamt that I painted myself orange to ward off cars that were veering off the road. I dreamt that, in springtime, I jumped off a cliff to prove my resilience and, luckily, landed in a lake. I began again. I knew I was meant to do something, but in life I was afraid, immobile, unsure. In the mirror I was a pebble, a stewed little bean. My mother explained how father had no soft spaces and his kindnesses were expended only on sharp objects. I thought about living in the city or helping shape fires on a farm. Then I decided to lift father in his sleep and move him into a line with others just like him until they all formed a wall and each one shouted, "I'm king of the stones."

3.   The sexy stranger that appeared wanted to do some bodily harm. Her legs flexed and kicked in all directions, her arms slashed here and there, her eyes cut me into too many little pieces. Soon she'd reach for a sword. A new world surrounded her. A moon pasted itself above the desolate landscape, a tower of mistakes, and a gate of skulls. A torture pit mapped out the territory. The terrible giants or the shriekers would soon arrive. My hand trembled then clicked and all those visceral, numerous threats were gone.

4.   The child was lost when the earthquake began. Her mother and father were near a fountain in the park scrutinizing a yellow bird that seemed happy when their daughter hopped toward a carousel, hid behind a fat tree. She heard her name being called for a while. When the girl turned around, her parents had disappeared suddenly. Something alarming was quickening in her stomach. The carousel horses jabbed one another. She could hear trees rumbling their shock and things broke around her. Buildings cracked and returned to their rock forms. The girl ran toward home as fast as she could, afraid the earth would split. She couldn't find her way, her familiar landmarks had vanished. The shaking quieted again, except for her heart beating furiously. At home her parents swept up broken pieces of their belongings, including the child's drinking glass etched with horses galloping in circles around it.

## Confessions of a Ventriloquist

Fear blazes lessons into our brain boxes and can make us enact silly things. I used to be afraid of doing book and literary readings although, as a child, I'd performed show tunes in front of anyone who would watch me. At my graduate school thesis reading I stood outside the door and asked everyone entering if they really wanted to go in there. I have gradually and slowly overcome that paralysis after trying the drug propranolol and breaking down the components of a reading and rehearsing them. For a week or more before a reading I would hardly sleep or eat and, gradually, that time period shrank to the day before. Finally I'm able to sleep and eat beforehand. I have traced the difficulty to my mother's criticism but I am still desensitizing it.

I recently watched a video of a seal that threw itself inside a nearby motorboat and huddled there while several orca whales circled the boat, waiting. I'm still talking to my dead cat although sometimes I use my words to address the elderly stray cat. I know exactly how my dead cat would respond but I'm not sure about the stray one. I'm speaking to my former cat, yet the conversation is actually between myself and myself, a bit like "Psycho."

Right now I'm using my mother's internalized voice to criticize parts of myself, my puffy stomach, my graying hair, my inability to write something decent. Am I absorbing those that like or dislike me and are close to me? Sometimes an utterance appears inside my mind unexpectedly and forcefully.

"Make me." She did.
I disguise myself.
Complaints are marinating in a wooden bowl.
Nobody can touch those lies that become true.
What are those strange gray things?
You are melting into someone with the same name.
I said what I didn't know, becoming my mother.
I'm two things, one I've overcome.

# Ghost Notes

# Irrevocable

Death is a skeleton riding a white horse (like love) holding a black and white flag. The Tarot card represents change, transformation, transition. My dead cat, Cyrus, and dead father are insertions then subtractions. They evolved from living creatures to memories to ideas to feelings. I hold on. The past is far away, starting to collect like dust on everything and colored by experience, death a comparison. Sometimes there is death and sometimes there is addition, a box of air, earth drifting round and round, voyaging senses. And then everything changes.

I have placed a barrier so that I don't have to think about my own death until it's imminent. I hope to be alive one moment and gone the next because I'm a worrier. I will step farther, going backwards, until I finally fall off the roof. The knowing is the most difficult.

My first experience of death was flushing my pet baby alligator down the toilet where I hoped he would be reunited with other alligators in the sewers. Now I am still questionable, unhinged. Death is in much that I write as renewal, a plot device, or the conclusion of a character. It makes the world feel paper-thin, the grazing of two different materials against one another. Yet people kill themselves in so many ways, relationships and situations that erupt until someone feels too much, even a sunless winter or a sad song with an opportunistic guitar, an endless cause, synchronization, someone who knows better but is weary and desires nothing.

I like being in a quiet room for a long time. It seems death-like in its own way, but it is the opposite, a coffin flourishing, rest kaleidoscoping. I need silence and time to write. My childlessness and difficulties and criticism of myself are symptoms.

Statistics on anyone's longevity are individual based on sex, race, current age, height, weight, fitness, life events (income, education, marital status etc.) and lifestyle choices (consumption of tobacco or alcohol) but generally the average 65 year old male can expect to live to 87 and female to 89. (*Time.com*, *"How Long Will You Live?" 10/10/14*).

Death is a shock, even when expected, a mistake, or the stealing of something that you had offered someone already at a low price. You return to your room, unlocking it, and find it empty. There is an industry to deal with the bodies. Saudade is described as the love that is left when the object of that love is gone, a cacophony of sound gone silent, still echoing. (*Wikipedia*, *"Saudade"*). Even with people brought back to life, we don't know what happens to us in death. Religions try to explain death and the afterlife. People who died and returned to life generally describe a personal heaven or hell but scientists say it's the brain box deprived of oxygen.

# Absence of

I blame too much on outmoded bodies. Can't we evolve into more spiritual beings, straddling this world and whatever is next? A better house for our souls? For example, the "Great Chain of Being" is a hierarchical structure involving all life and matter, beginning with God and ending with stones and minerals. It was important in Elizabethan, Renaissance, and Enlightenment thought (*Arthur Lovejoy, The Great Chain of Being, Harvard U Press, 1970*). Epigenesis is focused on the human mind as the center of creativity and development. (*Wikipedia, "Spiritual Evolution"*).

Components of death:
*Ghosts*, accumulating in a hat or elbow or moving pencils or chairs
*Bones*, reciting the names for what has been dismantled and left in the spaces between sky and earth
*Dust*, the past and the future
*Memories*, that take us elsewhere

What happened to all that beauty with its cold hands? The soul could be what happens when we stop consuming uncertainty, a small, red rain inside a body.

What to remember: we are all dying a tiny bit every day and a gift-shaped space haunts a wall.

Remember to laugh although you were only asleep. Breathe in, then out.

# Ghost Notes

I see my dead cat again in his usual places, even though I'm taking care of an elderly stray. A ball of undisguised light crawling across a floor distracts, makes me think it's something living. I become attentive. It squeezes, condensing my heart less and less. I'm accustomed to his staccato ghost, summarizing the parts of his life that I knew. There's a certain kind of loneliness for an animal. I feel experimental. I dreamt I was having sex with my husband when a bird flew inside our bedroom and tangled itself irrevocably in my hair.

The bones curving around my shoulders ache. When my grandfather died, my back hurt as I tried to avoid my usually absent father and his girlfriend, who was my age, at the funeral. It was his father, with his gnarled heart, in the box that would slowly turn to dust. They wanted me to be with them in their car to the cemetery. But I wasn't interested in getting to know either one of them. Later the woman became his wife, then left him, and he found another. My father's heart failed him in the same way his own father's had except that my father was sitting and watching floating bodies in the background glow of a television. I was something to grasp and put aside and perhaps next in the familial line of having my heart disappoint me.

Too many artist friends have died aortically young, often from accidents or cancer. My writer friends have fared better, living longer. As I grow older my infirmities greet me primitively and rhetorically, a broken bone in my left foot, a lost fallopian tube, half my thyroid. I don't have anything chronic. I splurge forward.

Me: A sea of words to entertain you?
Death: Don't be lackadaisical.
Me: How about some tea or lemon cake? You know I resemble several other people.
Death: A mood must come over me.
Me: Ignore me.
Death: Something doubtful in me just undoubted itself.
Me: How far back do we go?
Death, laughing: This is easy.
Death, seriously: What do you think?
Me: That I've known you all my life.

## Finally, First Person

The doctors told my husband's father that he had six months to live because of lung cancer and a sarcoma they had operated on and could no longer treat. They placed him with hospice services. Six months later hospice told him, "Call us when you need us." It's been almost three years. He is a contentedly cheerful person who adores his wife, reading newspapers, and programming his multiple VCRs. He has not changed into someone else. He just became more of who he already was.

I'm reading another book by someone long dead. I enjoy art by people who are no longer living. Much of my furniture was made by someone in their prime sixty years ago.

The dead don't stay dead. They change our minds. We have conversations with them, imagine new situations, extrapolate since there are lots of rooms in our minds and lots of places to hide secrets. We argue.

The future:
airy shoes and warm autobiographical food
hair growing ungovernably

everyone else is correct about me
trading in my childhood for apples
my thoughts are today's implications
affectionate sexual reconstructions
my teeth are equivocal, unsure about staying
I have a mouthful of verdicts yet my pants wander
my feet have become inappropriate
bodies, like day becoming night, impress us

Oh Death,
You are funny. Oh so funny. We met at an outdoor party late one night, behind a tree where my boyfriend and I had disturbed tree leaves, ferns, flowers, grass, mingling them, making them into other shapes and then smearing our bodies with the mixture. Pain and pleasure tickled me when I rode him. Yes, I drank too much, swiveling away from the out-held arms of tall dark trees that said, *We are inside out*, repeatedly. I liked to run in the dark, trying to avoid odd, dangerous things licked by moonlight that reminded me of other humorous things. I was useable. Rocks viewing our awkwardness made me think of gods judging us. But we aren't sedentary stones. We move and giggle and die on our own. We calibrate ourselves and our wants and what we can and can't do. I did it. I died because the world was inside me too much. A joke: the difference between sex and death is that with death you do it alone and no one laughs at you. For me it's humorous, for you it's…

# Part III
# The Etiquette of Space

# Everything is Everything Else

# Everything is Everything Else

The promise of something new dangles, new house, new cat, same old husband and life, which are quite good. A renewal. The death of my cat lingers, bedraggles into an accomplice. The elderly stray cat that kneads and rearranges my hair to calm himself and my ninety year old mother, who dislikes my graying hair because it ages her, disagree about my hair for their own particular reasons.

My husband is an identical twin. He and his brother weren't lonely when they were young. They shorthanded a language between them, built trains and Lincoln Logs together, shot eight millimeter movies, joined the Rocket Club. One bucket of water spilled into two. Now they are rumors of themselves, physically different, changed by life. They reside in separate states and are growing closer to one another again. They both see the possibilities in ludicrous cats. One has studied insects, the other old electronic equipment. They both enjoy musical instruments, and they both like cities. I believe they are lonely for each other and fulfill one another the way buttons slip into their allotted holes to hold a shirt together. I, too, have seen my doppelganger, briefly, when I was about ten years old, at an ice skating rink. I was surprised that there was a girl who looked just like me. I wondered what her life was like then. Now I wonder what her life has become and how different we look.

My elderly cat that I'd tended to for sixteen years died a few months ago and an elderly stray has disjointedly married us. While the stray repeats certain gestures of my beloved cat, he is more broken and wary, a creature wanting to stay for a while and leave versus one attentive in a nearby resting place. The stray has retained many habits, none are ours. I try to sift through all the people I am and find one to complement him. But it is a two way street and our puzzle pieces don't fit together yet, so he is a reminder of what I once had.

I'm still awaiting a new house, one full of serious things, sunlight, silence, speech, books. A specific desire can reside within a larger desire, shaping it. I want a mostly empty house with enormous windows and a husband with long hair and sneakers. I could be someone else, discarding my minor afflictions, my exterior aging, someone speaking loudly, with thoughts racing up and down corridors, someone excited as light pushes aside a curtain, someone arriving at both the future and past simultaneously.

Every moment is juxtaposed on another, future onto the past, future onto the present, past onto the future, etc. My grandparents' apartment in New York City had a living room with thick plastic covering every available seat, sofa, and chair. Perpetually new furniture because of disuse, it was one of those ironies of life, not living in the living room. I wanted to be elsewhere. My grandparents' habits had trickled down to them from an old time in another country where everything needed to be preserved. With no place to sit and relax, I disappeared, asleep yet awake. I agreed with my father's parents. There was too much death and decay in the world and I wanted to be alive while I was still alive.

## After those warnings I didn't know what to say

Twenty seven years married and twenty six in the same Seattle house and three cats have come and gone. I'm gentled and distracted as I speak to my recently dead cat inside my head in the shower, scruffy yard, gazing at a friend's colorful saltwater aquarium, on a bus moving my inert body from here to there. I'm listing all that can go wrong with motherhood: caring too much; caring too little; criminal mischief, as in digging a hole where there wasn't one before; subtler elegies like tattoos; who broke what; why the color blue causes a frenzy; how to survive being in the wrong place at the right time. I notice the bed where my cat left the shape of his body. I still don't want to imitate my mother who is a storm to my seasonal weather. If I'd been loved by my mother would I still be a writer? Would I be who I am now? I like children and dogs. I have neither. I like silence. I deserve the amiable ghost I am, not the mother I think I might have been.

Missing the baby who:
makes butterflies kneel on the sky
peels the painted faces of his mother and father
lives in a place called sleep where bones speak
puts his white wings on over his coat
grows larger except for his hands
is clumsy with contingencies
runs toward shadows
smiles at unbroken oceans that remind him of a resting body
kisses a question when no one is looking
points at the one god I've never noticed
frowns at clouds that fall from his fingers

## Where are the others?

Sometimes different parts of my body fidget or ache for no reason other than stress. One day will my doppelganger take my place? Would I take hers? I like the feel of murder without the murdering. I need a push toward someone but a child, a vague reproduction, was never the answer, even when I could have one. I'm restless in the perfunctory rituals of my life that appear to keep me safe but really can't. My only way to protest is to become someone else for a while, someone who can have experiences or absorb the experiences of others.

My books don't resemble children. I throw the unsatisfactory ones away, ones with insufficient plots or characters, ones that fail to wring me out. Books can't act or grow or change into what the world can view and absorb but they can incite readers to do so. The new books I write chart my internal and external transformations, as if recording a child's different heights with marks on a wall. Do we notch the wall when we shrink with age, unspooling life? When I reread my books, as well as old favorites, their meaning is different.

Growing up in New York City made me anonymous. I could become another person on a bus, a street, in a store. As a brown-eyed teenager with ridiculously long brown hair to my waist I became an orphan or a wild girl with six brothers or a shyly studious girl depending on my mood or the stranger I was speaking to. We see parts of ourselves in parts of others and those are the traits that we usually dislike the most.

A few nights ago I dreamt that my agitated twin, into whom I poured my worry and my worst feelings and inclinations, who studied me condescendingly yet with sympathy, snapped my neck. It was a relief.

The child:
ambles into rooms I've forgotten inside me
anticipates what he wants with unclenching fists
ignores me, stitching my regrets in and out of his skin while he's sleeping
ignores me, doing and undoing his clothes before a mirror
ignores me, while he considers all his beckoning, internally lit cities
tiptoes through the seasons, afraid of being snagged by something decaying
allows his heart to hiccup his body into being
parades his tattooed half woman/half bird in another house with abbreviated
motions
disappears into his own world in which these things could suddenly happen

## Partially Hidden

My husband's twin brother's wife has early onset Alzheimer's, which began when she was fifty five, and he adjusts and adjusts. They live in Indianapolis. She lost the face she had yesterday and the day before that, and the day before that. Her sky grows smaller, folding itself away from disuse. He doesn't have a lot of choices. His wife has forgotten how to tie her shoes, shower, sign her name, and she's recently forgotten what stairs are for. He likes to travel but can't leave her alone.

They don't have children either. But he is patient and repeats everything to her innumerable times since she keeps asking the same questions. He shops, cooks, cleans, works, takes care of the yard, and now tries to bath her and soon, perhaps, feed her. She is his child. She had been difficult in the past and may become more so. She follows him everywhere, including the bathroom, not wanting to be alone with what's left of herself.

My doppelganger arrives from a world that is sentimental about needs, every noise is about life and every thought becomes a form of music. I ask her, "Which one of us cries?" "Which one had the dream about a place that was full and green?" I think about explaining what it's like to be a woman who can be alone or silent or one who is shrinking into smaller and smaller spaces or one who avoids shadows and crowds. But she might already know. And I want to know more about her. If she feels people's eyes stab into her or remembers a dog who likes to hide its face under her hands. "What is this body?" I want answers. "And what do we do with it?" I'm not sure she'll understand, especially if she's like me inside. I wonder whether someone seeing us for the first time would be able to see our likenesses and differences or whether they would simply turn away.

## It's likely that something is happening

Today I'm an animal waiting for moonlight to move me, muffling my words, carving my sentences like initials in a tree. I'm bereft of children. I merge my exhalations with my husband's breath in a city that traps shadows behind emerging buildings. I perplex my mother and use the monotonous language of cicadas with my sister. I'm in a boat, refusing to float on a startled sea with my dead father. I water withered plants. I can lure water into the shape of a glass. I feel misplaced by rain, which already knows too much about me, which might think it is me.

# Lopsided

# Lopsided

I live in a world of my making. News reaches me and crawls away to make space for more; a cat resides there, maybe the ghost of my former cat, or a stray sleeping with my husband; I prune plants in order to see the foldable cloud-filled sky; houses transpose themselves, one on top of another, growing taller; people and writing strum my emotions, searching; work is scattered, less specific; I enjoy muddled dancing (ballet). In Seattle, rain is my radio and the moon has fluttered elsewhere. A story is the only way to make sense of the contradictions, the conflation of the best and the worst.

Last night I dreamt about my familiar, tiny town, which I don't believe exists, unless I've seen it one time, briefly, years ago. But it's more likely an amalgamation of towns I've seen in my lifetime. This ideal town is about ten blocks long with mediocre houses and a few storefronts. Revisited in my dream, this half rural/half city is growing rapidly, structures becoming larger and fatter, with a new gleam to my dream town's sheen, which appears empty although I somehow know all the houses are occupied.

My husband reminds me of what needs to be done daily and what is waiting outside our front door. I become tired and isolated, my eyes and ears weakening as I age. My friends and I wander through Seattle streets and events, unsure what we're searching for. Sometimes we fabricate a quest for dark chocolate or coffee or tea, an excuse for discovering a play, film, or book or restaurant or something specific like a visit to the Georgetown Steam Plant to see industrial pipes and equipment or the Ferris wheel for a water view. Do I long for someplace else because the outside world is unlike my inside one? Is my inside world more peaceful? Outside moonlight highlights tree branches and parts of buildings and wind steals shadows, returning them as objects. Puddles ache for birds and feel no pain when they arrive. Woods cough up leaves. People I trust return again and again like former pets materializing refurbished.

# A Hidden Story

Someone was lurching around a forest where trees slumped as they thought about darkness. This man was seeking a fortune or a secret or perhaps he had once hidden something from himself that he was attempting to find. He circled until he found a spot where a fern sprouted delicate green leaves and a rock collected declarations. He began digging. He penetrated the gap between thinking about something and doing it and the one between what his life was and what he thought it should be. He dug all the way to the other side of the world.

# A Story about Memories

A woman grew lopsided because of a man who had abandoned her. Her desire for him pulled her body to one side. She limped. She needed new scenery. She knew she would eventually have to make room in herself for someone she didn't know yet. But first she decided to try anything to get the man back since he was rapidly becoming another one of her memories. She tried love potions, prayers, and asking advice from friends who became tired of her insistences and eventually stopped being her friend. Days passed. The woman felt compelled into a deep ocean by small, tugging waves of emotion. She toppled underwater one day at a beach. She died fighting with water, replacing one thing with another.

# An Introvert's Guide to Other Places

When I first visited my husband's house, before he was my husband, he had pinned a sign on his front door that said, "This is the place." And many years later I know that it was.

Several months before, I had divorced my first husband, serving him papers at the restaurant he had started in Missoula, Montana. He had grown desperate for money, gambled, and liked drugs, but he kissed me as if he was first meeting me every time. I had grown anxious, dreaming I was naked and taking a test at school or nervously trying to repair a broken watch. We had "irreconcilable differences." There was sorrow, if not for the man, then for the dream our marriage had represented.

Why move to Seattle? Life was slower, easier in Missoula, but there I knew everyone I could date, a self-contained place rimmed by puckered, snowy mountains whose inversions caused terrible winter pollution. Seattle stroked me with rain, its views of attainable islands and abundance of foreign movies and books and plays. Everything was larger, busier, and there I, hopefully, wouldn't mistake sex, kindness, or neediness for love again.

Other worlds include:
a long illness you think you're done with but you're not
imitating a preventative marriage
strays that ask for little, with repeated disappearances
interruptions that belong somewhere else
costuming the heart
a murderous mouth close to an ear
jittery ghosts with ruined faces and recriminations
every blade of grass, every leaf
children purring with their small voices
stumbling toward the moon's gravitational bones.

Dreamtime involves totem symbols reminding Australian aborigines that a person's ancestors accumulate all knowledge. And everyone's ancestors are as one. Dreaming begins before a person is born and continues after their lifetime. (*Encyclopedia Britannica, "The Dreaming," the Editors, 7/20/98*).

Forces that deplete or enhance our worlds can move someplace where our ghosts don't know where to find us, protecting our words from others, a yellow bird alighting on snow, the breaking of stiff, white china. Some days I need to rest and shore myself up for what will arrive from the world I live in.

When I was a teenager I had no interest in the older, wealthy men who drove fast cars that resembled smudges of color as they moved. My mother wanted me to date them. They didn't care about me. They wanted what they wanted. My mother jealously hid, behind a glass door in the lobby of our New York City apartment building, watching me leave in an expensive car.

Please no more:
sounds near twitching trees like something dying
cobwebbed shadows whose symptoms include sudden interrogations and night wakings
prayers without alternate colors or sky
outside noise rubbing inside noise rubbing body noise
rugged winters with their instructions for oblivion
time hidden in insects and water

This morning I watched a squirrel scrabble across a long telephone line, quickly yet halting to assess its situation in the air. A blade of grass forgets its place in a lawn because it's surrounded by so many others and so much is happening around it. There are distractions but what are these things replaced with?

When something is wrong with one part of my body I'm aware of the rumor of the rest of it. I carry my own shadows. But I need to see farther to places that are significant, Paris, Rome, Newfoundland, Falkland Islands, Montana, New York, Tampa, Poland, New Zealand, Galicia. My landmarks include: clouds like white hats atop Mt. Rainier; the spidery Eiffel Tower; the parts of Mt. St. Helens that are left; certain buildings in Seattle that remind me of a deodorant ball, boxes, eyelids, or intestines; a white beach in Greece; a square and cemetery in Prague; Gaudi in Spain; bird-like flowers in Hawaii; the arterial water-filled canals of Venice; Golden Gardens beach park and the old cobblestone parts of Ballard.

What I remember most: dead leaves nuzzling everything; diaphanous artwork inside new museums; a boiler room, a city of pipes on a navy ship; water rippling while someone is crying; a giant, outdoor cowboy hat and boots; invisible patterns only seen on paper because of fire or water; a room full of raindrops; geraniums in a row like a red blindfold; the moon jumping from roof to roof; loitering seasons; and the buildings I navigate by in Seattle, which keeps changing.

## When Worlds Collide

Often my mother unspooled me from my childhood/adolescent sleep in the middle of the night with her chant, "Nobody loves me." I would awaken, go into the sunken apartment living room and she would talk while we watched Johnny Carson. Towards morning she offered me one of her sleeping pills and I usually stayed awake after I swallowed it, feeling a compelling tug and release of my consciousness. She usually suggested I skip school but I liked school. I discovered I could sleepwalk through life.

My imaginary twin unobtrusively does what she wants, buoyantly dreaming of a ship sailing to Cuba. Or disliking the paradox of a happy room in which sad stories are written, she will transform it into a library. She insults people who have insulted her. She shapes her world to herself, to her desires, reshaping it as light fills a room and is later gone, as though she drank a liquid world and it fit itself within her body. She is unlike other people and they generally don't like her, finding her raw and too wild.

The man stole necessary items, red apple pies, corroded jars of sun tea, kitchen towels, cans of unfathomable meat or alphabet soup which entertained him with its letters. He weaved through shedding trees in his shabby clothes to the miniscule lawns and insufficient, flimsy houses. He lived under a small bridge connecting land slung onto each side of a river the color of old dried peas and the shape of a tongue. He ran back to his box of toothpaste, his toothbrush, comb, powder, a frayed blanket, a shirt, underwear tucked behind a rock. But it was gone. His hair whipped his head as it spun around in the waning light. He saw the other man picking at his teeth with an Army knife, listening to a worn radio by the dirty water near his box. The man unsheathed his knife. He rushed toward the man who stood and stared at him as if he was something from another world.

Uncivilization

# Uncivilization

I want to be lost in an internal wilderness because our planet has knees and elbows, a mind which resembles a teeming city, blood that recreates the noise of a relentless ocean, arterial veins, untamed hair, a vigilant skin through which we learn everything. I'm planning a trip to Iceland with friends where I would like the outdoor landscape to match what is happening inside me. When I'm outside myself, I watch my body adjust to bad habits, fretting over food, desolate decisions, my feeble attempts at friendship. I like the company of flames and ice. My heart beats a message in its cage of bone, saying *cool down to nothing, yet be awed by everything outside of you.* I lay my head on my husband's chest, listen to his heart emitting the sound a small animal makes when it is killed by another small animal just outside our window.

In Seattle I pour myself into things and people that don't last. We are a social species, needing to be shaken occasionally and reminded of transience. I believe it's the reason I'm afraid of tiny holes or tears in the thin membrane of my bedsheets, having caught a toe in one once as a child and, in my movements to extricate myself, ripped the sheet apart.

My husband and I recently visited his parents in Greensboro, North Carolina. In the airplane, flying above land that distantly resembled a green colored board game, I was fascinated by the clouds which were easily dispersed as we continued through them. I wanted to hopscotch from one to the other, if I could eliminate my too human weight. Viewed from the sides or from within, they were airy sculptures made from wisps of air.

We too are ephemeral.

We are too accustomed to the earth's revolutions, day/night (time), hot/cold (temperature), predicting the future and the seasons. I expect my recently dead cat to be where he usually is, waiting for me by the ridiculous, wet bathtub or peering eerily around a door. Because he isn't there, I'm now also anticipating his absence. Will another planet become our wilderness? Will another life form arise? The planets, including a few parts of our own, are untried and unknown. They are the new frontier, encompassing what is similar and familiar and their opposites, what is dissonant and frightening to us.

Planets in our solar system include:

- Mercury is slow, takes 88 days to orbit our sun, has a weak magnetic field, and no atmosphere.

- Venus is volcanic and spins slowly and is very hot.

- Mars orbits the sun in an eccentric circle, has two moons, and is cold, red, and dusty.

- Jupiter is large and massive and has rocks surrounded by a liquid hydrogen sea.

- Saturn is very hot and its rings are made of various ice particles resembling a woman wearing a large, expensive hat.
(*The Planets Today.com*, "*The planets of our solar system*")

## The Body's Dispute

Are our uncontrollable emotions transitory or do they linger in the body? Where do they go? I imagine our unwanted or unused feelings gathered into human shapes in a forest or another quiet, empty place to live. More and more accumulate and whole cities of them form, jostling to find some place with more space. We often don't enjoy our feelings and try to stuff them somewhere, shoulders, back, neck, stomach. Happiness and love are glorious if we can recognize them for what they are. Can I catch someone else's emotions, someone who is thrusting them on me or letting them loose between us? I have felt angry when someone is angry at me or joy around someone exuding joy. But I've learned that I'm not responsible for the emotions or actions of other people. This has taken me a long time to learn. In *Scientific American*, in an article by G. Lewandowski, Jr. called, "Is a bad mood contagious?" he calls this reaction "emotional contagion" and there is a three step process: first, nonconscious copying achieved by adjusting your posture, facial expression, and movement to match the other person; next, a feedback stage where a smile assumes contentment; lastly, synchronizing two individual's feelings and behaviors. Some animals, especially dogs, display emotional contagion.

Disobedience includes:
a moon crawling by, opening and closing stars
the dishonest woods throwing rocks in my path
loitering in the consciousness of a tree until its leaves fall
dogs chasing sunlight because it smells wrong
acting like an umbrella so I'll never be alone
rain making up stories so it can touch everyone
cats preferring the spot where a woman and a man once kissed
my shadow not understanding me yet it keeps on trying
my conversations including more people in them that I don't like
betraying you so you can absorb me into your body or your mind

## The Singing of Bones

I grew up in New York City but, when I was young, my family summered at a house in Westchester where I remember large trees, a variety of elegant butterflies, rabbits twitching near a stone fence, birds making the green leaves of bushes tremble. I remember my grandfather descending into a patch of poison ivy to retrieve a ball and returning unscathed. We stopped going to that house when the owner's son hung himself in the garage.

Some people that know me say that they are scared by my fiction books. "But you seem so nice," they say.    I believe there's a bit of horror and unpredictability in everything.  My husband can't read my books since he's sensitive to disturbing material.  I don't understand how he survives in today's world.

The wilderness is one way of connecting to something bigger than ourselves, something majestic we break into pieces like ice or our voices.  When I visit Golden Gardens beach, near where I live, I spoon bodies of water, oatmeal-colored sand, and the declarative sky inside me, and it calms me.

## Levitations, Posthumously

We mean well, nursing a baby bird that drops from a cloud-filled tree, like my neighbor that feeds all the nearby stray animals.  Nature displays her cruelty and loneliness in violent spurts.  My neighbor doesn't know what to do about the young raccoon perched in her tree, scaring the other partakers off from her offered food and the baby bird dies terrified.  Nature's difficult and unjust ways ensure its continuance.  But we, as a species, have withdrawn from its seemingly fickle and unfair bent, ignorant of what's necessary to sustain this world.

The world chooses. It complains. It tells us about fish, frogs, birds, ambitious streams, and the long-suffering trees in inscrutable increments.  We look down occasionally, as if we had just dropped a cup that shattered into pieces. Landscapes. We kick rocks from the edge of a cliff.  America likes to tame the untamed, enjoying its chaos at the same time. The new West is currently trying to save its parks and open areas. Think "Taming of the Shrew" in old England.  We like wind and cats, but not too much of them, and especially when they have unruly minds.  Some days I want to put on wildness like a jacket, do something I don't usually do to excess: drinking, smoking, sex, running, yelling at people, but then I fold up that urge and tuck it back into a drawer, explaining to myself that it is the feeling I need to recognize, that its idea doesn't need to be expressed. We live behind glass, behind civilization.

## Undependable Pastorals

I'm doing research for my winter trip to Iceland with my friends and I hope to find glaciers, waterfalls, volcanos, lakes, geysers, lava caves, Northern Lights. No tall trees.  Seattle already contains trees, textured water, rain, a circuitry of forests, mountains, hills, beaches, ferries.

I imagine shaky scenes, rehearse old age pirouettes in my head, think about a parakeet reincarnated as a woman, how she adored sunlight, hit her head on a lackadaisical ceiling. I annihilate myself, becoming a romantic, a hunter, a child, an angel, leaving my body, uninhabited, my blood still flowing, bones knitting, breath murmuring in and out. My words become sharper knives. Imagination is abundant, unlimited, an enhancement.

My wilderness has no windows or cupboards or mirrors. It doesn't sit, sleep, smile, knit, sew, watch television, move furniture. A wilderness dreams, likes abundant art for art's sake, suffers, transforms, enjoys a primordial silence, stitches light through metaphorical trees and embraces night through metaphorical grass, flowers through brightness and attachment, enhances past oblivions, growing whatever it can wherever it can, shrinking with time, and regret. It never knows what will happen. It considers other people's ideas, which are often larger and more predatory.

## Bjorn's Icelandic Saga

Bjorn was brave as tree roots, a hunter in the dark, an heir to unnumbered winds. He depended on duty and light, wedded as he was to indolence and the inadvertent snow. He surveyed his beloved land, blood in his mouth. His cold, shifting knees creaked. He needed a wife. Olafur's daughter's eyes met his over a feast, then over a fire. The small of her back was strong, tall, inviting. Olafur had asked Bjorn to clear one of his fields, then to catch an intelligent fish, which was offered to Olafur's family. Then there was the hurtful sword fight with Egil, who also liked Olafur's daughter. After Egil's death Olafur's daughter went blind. Bjorn married her although it became difficult for him to look at his sheep, horses, or land.

**Always Choose Beauty**

## Always Choose Beauty

Beauty was a dog that my family and I owned a long time ago, when I was almost a teenager and my sister was four years younger. The dog was a black miniature poodle whose eyes reflected a single mother and her two daughters. Later, near death, when pain filled her and blood bubbled from her sweet nose and mouth, her curly dark extravagant fur and calmness unfolded inside me, relentlessly stayed. I think of a woman flogging dirt out of a rug or a man beating the limbs of a dogwood with a baseball bat to rejuvenate its lost blooms. Something could be revived in another form, the lovely grass over a dog's body, a sapling brimming with large white blossoms.

## Collectibles

As a woman, an older one, I have had narrowly defined historical roles in cultural America, family and food, nurturing, sex appeal. Women were considered blind and deaf to certain problems but, hopefully, provided for. Then came the vote, the sexual revolution, and now, even though no one explains to me who I am, I know the first thing everyone glimpses is the vessel. Some people are more interested in becoming what or who others want, polished, harvested, painted, and sculpted into a particular creation.

Why not use what you have? Don't be a shadow but the shape that makes it. My mother likes to be looked at, a woman poured into high heels, ladled with men's attention and money. She's almost ninety, and still tangled in images and preconceived ideas. What kind of person is that? And what's inside a good girl? A necklace of apologies, dissolving long legs, dreamy feathers, a silver antique saltshaker, a husband's slack mouth, an intrusive cell phone, a white fringed shirt, a tablecloth embroidered with a loveable snake, a secret tattoo uncovered like an outburst.

Beauty tips:
Think of a sentimental story and adjust your face accordingly.
Don't spill anything from your body, made mostly of water.
Stuff something new inside.
Your hunger awaits.

## The Beholder

Beauty says it can do things it can't, transfiguring arms into chairs, befriending wrinkles and scars, finding gestures in mechanical objects. Beauty, and its claims, can be ignored or minimized, but I remember stumbling into a certain vast vertical ray of sunlight that reached down like a ladder from Seattle clouds or a bright red geranium staring back at me. Accidents make me feel alive, that stunning moment of recognition, frozen in a specific place and time. All I can see is that rectangular light or a shocking flower. Without the wreckage of time and the way it dissolves everything would we acknowledge or cherish beauty? True beauty doesn't know it is beautiful. Beauty, the dog, didn't last forever, but we'll never forget how she stared at the sun peeking through an apartment window, evaluating the weather outside. We take instruction the best we can from life like trees huddling to find more than they need, trying to find what surprises them into tree happiness.

A day is juxtaposition, context, and it often involves concealment in order to discover or create something charming. A puzzle, made of many parts, blurs the lines between beautiful things. It is complete when everything lines up just right.

Is there beauty in everything and we simply need to find it? This is the romance of seeing but everyone is different. One man likes tall, thin women with proper shoes and another man likes large women with chiseled features who wear brightly colored clothes and who talk to anyone that will listen. Ugliness has its place too. It's the underbelly, the usual product of life and hard times. It is everywhere and varied.

Beauty wants to be serious, so she grows more limbs.

Beauty doesn't like being left alone at the beach on a towel.

Beauty doesn't need to know names.

Beauty is idle and forgets facts.

Beauty is crazy about the color blue.

Beauty is attentive to signs and explanations and misses your cold white hands.

Beauty stares at the clouds and nearly falls off a roof.

Beauty laughs and then comes towards a decision about the moon.

Beauty introduces herself all day long.

## Still Life with Autobiographical Snow

It's winter in Iceland and I vacationed in Reykjavik for nearly a week with two friends. I believe in personal frontiers. I have reverence for natural beauty and its placating effects. However, we found tourists at nearly every site we visited, and the Aurora Borealis was green smudges of vaguely moving light in the night sky. The one time I saw the Northern Lights unintentionally in Missoula, Montana it was a spectacular, undulating blanket of bright lights. I still had a wonderful time in Reykjavik and the surrounding areas. The vast, sparse landscape filled me like a religion. I saw long, quavering waterfalls stretched out over cliffs, geysers that squirted regularly like dependable hearts, a black rock beach with toothy basalt columns, a warm lagoon seeking out its shape, geothermally heated water in the pipes with its rotten egg smell, mountains with white scarfs of snow, rivers sobbing along rocks, diminutive Icelandic horses with overlong bangs, swathes of volcanic ground with moss or snow, and squat, stark little trees.

A harsh cold slapped our faces and made it hard to breathe. Does beauty require silence and worship? Perhaps, because it is stunning some people want to possess it, perhaps mistaking it for love.

## Long Ago the Future was Different

The past knew our names and faces and had bad dreams concerning what was happening inside us. Sometimes what is dreamt comes to life like a woman whose hair becomes fur and spreads all over her body. This is called hypertrichosis, dubbed the werewolf syndrome. Julia Pastrana worked in a circus in the 19th century and Alice Doherty, called "The Minnesota Woolly Baby," was born in 1887. They were grim, lovely, odd, and poorly treated. (*mental floss, "8 Very Hairy People," Miss Cellania, and show history, "Alice Doherty"*).

There are breeds of dogs, Chinese Crested, English Bull Terrier, The Komondor, and Mexican Hairless, that are so strange looking they become adorable and fascinating. We too are dichotomous, good/evil, female/male, sad/happy, ugly/beautiful and all the gray areas in between. That is what makes me who I am, world-weary, driven, sometimes hurried into further being. It is winter somewhere and summer somewhere else. Mermaids, minotaurs, centaurs, satyrs, harpies, sirens, and all the other hybrid, half, or partially human creatures represent our divided selves. The things I'm told about myself can't be undone, those wayward thoughts, how to decide my appearance, how that transforms over time.

## Selling Beauty

I'm repeatedly told how to improve myself, occasionally subtly, often directly. Apparently I'm in dire need of amelioration and many friendly companies can aid me. I'm guaranteed levitation, a new disguise, attention from every direction, my questions made into novel temptations, men can be enveloped by my spells, my odors will improve, my teeth whiten, my hair dazzle, my breath become luminous, my figure triumphantly slim, and my face gorgeous. My beloved dead cat will spring back to life at the sight of me.

In my youth I worked at department stores most summers. The first retail store was my father's in Brooklyn and it specialized in bridal wear. My father fired me because of a fight he had with my mother, who was divorcing him. Both my mother and grandmother had been models. I was never pretty enough to draw that dream toward me, and I already knew what it looked like. An extraordinary face could skew a camera or make the too human hands behind it shake. It was a dream that could lay down with anyone. My mother and father lay down with other people for years. My sister and I didn't understand what had hovered between our parents to keep them together. My mother moved on and married three other men, my father two other women. I continued in my summers to work at larger, self-absorbed, well-stocked, famous department stores that sold more than clothes and accessories. I liked the dressing room mirrors that showed everything in triptych. Three mouths. Six eyes. As if I could choose. Three noses. So many eyebrows. My puzzling self in the way.

# In/Out Side

What if love was a commodity you could buy and sell like money? Could I fit the ghost of my cat or a person inside and carry it/them around with me? How long does it take the world to discover the truth about a person or situation? Why does the body love something different than the mind? Tell me your impossible facts.

Not everything is what it seems. That woman is much older than she appears. My beloved cat has been dead for a year although I still talk to him. Something was blurted out over the dinner table that was both mean and tantalizing. The sushi photographed in a magazine is composed of plastic. Pieces fall apart, and then I try to fit them back together.

When in doubt I go to my garden, which is duplicitous in its burgeoning, fading, drying, then dying back. Like the rest of us, it is momentary and contrary. I made numerous mistakes until I learned what each plant needed. I enjoyed viewing the first white snowdrops, shrugging tulips, odorous freesia and wisteria, the mesmerizing fuchsia and lavender, red leaves filling up the Japanese maples.

No more arguing about beauty. Just view a perfectly made object, a telescope, a tube, a lens, or a fossil embedded with something that had once been alive. All those shapes rise toward me and I'm painting myself painting.

# We Can Talk about That

# We Can Talk about That

I listened to ice melting in Iceland, a dessert fork flung against a plate, the hoarse noise my old stray cat makes when he wants to go outside, a personal earthquake rattling down our street like a truck. Still the world can shrink to a country, a state, a street, or a kitchen. A neighbor, who forgot her mind, once said, "It's nice that you're here, in the park with me." We were standing in her old, yellow, crooked kitchen that seemed to be dissolving in the afternoon light.

Loss and redemption has fur. Having lost one cat and gained another I stumble onward, learning how to wander, avoiding the homeless people living under a Seattle bridge near me. A man, who speaks to himself, not into a device, erects a complete bed with an iron frame, frayed sheets, covers, and a lumpy pillow. The man has long, stringy hair. He smiles. Holding out a dirty hand he says, "Here's a room where my heart was." A woman, with a face like a leaf, wearing a crocheted shawl, sits on her pile of clothes and bedding, with her pants legs spread apart, under noise and small light from the bridge above that opens occasionally. Sometimes a muscular bonfire burns, its arms reaching high into the air.

Many things I imagine don't come true, a swarm of bees emptying out a favorite restaurant so I can dine undisturbed, or lightning pointing in an expedient direction. I embrace imagination, some odd animal dangling from a tree branch, which, without my intervention, could fall and create a life of its own.

There is the economic value attributed to a life through a wrongful death lawsuit (someone's earning potential) or the value of a statistical life, as in: how much more to spend to save how many people? See the tobacco, auto, workplace, healthcare, clean air, or transportation industries. In the U.S. in 2008 $50,000 is the equivalent amount of money for one quality year of life. (*Time, "The Value of a Human Life, $129,000," Kathleen Kingsbury, 5/20/08*).

How much is an animal's life worth? What a human wants to spend on it.

Possessions:
a serious green striped jacket on someone's shoulders
a train moving slowly to gather a last look at yellow corn, chattering geese, and trees knitting themselves together above a river
quick, white wings that throw gulls into the air
emptiness that I try on when you are gone
singing into a vast silence of knotted clouds
doing arithmetic in the middle of winter
the defeated rise not thinking about themselves
what I am I leave

# Disturbed Dictionary

My mother's fur coats are made up of various parts of sharp-toothed animals. She has three different types: mink, fox, and something exotic I can't name. All of them need to be packed into cool, dark storage in the summer. Furs require breathable cloth, not plastic bags. They need space, and no direct humidity or sunlight. As clothing, they are more mausoleum than zoo.

It's Fall and the animals at the Seattle zoo, in their contradictory pastorals, are being fed their inscrutable futures. The Northern Trail area is jealous of the warm, steamy African Savanna or Tropical Rain Forest or Tropical Asia. The various sections of the zoo are the Trail of Vines for the orangutans, apes, monkeys, and a chilly, rugged landscape for bears, otters, goats, and owls, and an Australian type of habitat for kangaroos and emus. Birds are contained inside the enclosed Willawong Station, fluttering everywhere, landing on a shoulder or arm. A dome in the Tropical Rain Forest helps keep the vegetation inside damp and sweating. The Temperate Forest, which is similar to Seattle's landscape, contains Asian cranes, pandas, wolves. Life is a theme park.

I'm lonely at the zoo, watching a litany of flamingos leisurely fighting, furtively fucking, momentarily gliding over water with their passionate orange-pink and white feathers. They flap folded wings, stand on one impossibly long, slender leg, survey their scumbled enclosure while the sky unfurls over them. They are consumed with petty divisions, fights, and alliances. I think of my mother's words this morning, never nested close to enough, and all that's passed between us without beaks or claws or webbed feet. I remember the flamingos' large, pale eggs from last summer and wonder what the birds have grown into. I wonder at their wanting.

Our eyes lock between glass, the orangutan and me. She's in her exhibit, vines, earth, trees, torn burlap bags, and I'm in mine, cement, signs and explanations, artificial lights. Mine is temporary. Her eyes contain old ideas, upward and downward scenes, shadows and moonlight, overturned meat and scavenged vegetables, frayed, secretive objects, sunlight and unweaving the woven, scratched and smoothed fur, long grass tipping every which way, something frightening at night. Her dreams must be faster and more visceral than mine. We study each other's bodies and faces and slight movements. I speak, simply saying *Hello, beautiful.* No one else is there. She languidly looks at me, perhaps waiting for more words or waiting for nothing more than time to pass. I press my palm against the glass in front of her, and it is a long time before she raises her own, quickly taps the glass with her fingertips then turns to leave.

Tired women, usually in groups, are pushing strollers, disturbing leaves, which are collapsed everywhere. Small ambulatory children are excited, racing toward glass windows filled with animal antics or emptied landscapes. I'm sad for the lonely black and white tapir, a creature to himself, and I'm glad for the companionship between two hippos, whose backs surface regularly like giant, amiable rocks. At the Petting Farm, goats, with their blank, startled yet accepting faces, are positioned on table tops to nibble on twigs held out to them by volunteers. Pigs are writhing in hay, fancy chickens are pecking at soil. Strange miniature horses stare at their fences, and a rabbit, made of muscle and fur, waits curled patiently.

Vestiges of animals remain in me, like the desire to swat an insect at my knee. My cloud-white bones test their hard testimony. Fur is no longer visible, useable limbs, the belief that I'm talking only to myself, circling round and round my favorite places before I lie in them. I feel danger on the surface of circumstances, share incipient eyes, heads, hearts, and a reliance on scenery. We are more alive when fighting, yet none of us likes lions racing toward us out of nowhere. When I come home, I notice crows, hummingbirds, and gulls, cats and dogs, gray squirrels, possum, raccoons, frogs and insects, wondering exactly how they belong to us.

## Forgotten Constructions

I'm lifting my spoon repeatedly from hot soup to my mouth on a cold day. Pale, round stones fill my mouth. I'm shoving moons between my lips like a wolf. I'm lucky, eating when I want. A house surrounds me, shifts, stirs, and I'm safe from what roams the earth. I'm a flawed human, Hominin clade, using tools and complicated clothing, a strangled or robust fire to cook my food, with art and technology to express myself. At Halloween I usually dress as a black cat, flimsy velvet ears on a headband, a dark raggedy tail pinned above my buttocks. One quick motion and my costume flies off. Mostly, we've forgotten where we come from in our push to inhabit and relegate.

Totems:

I have become lost in a spider's web, the gelatinous, stringy material washing my hands, but I'm afraid of the tiny, devious spider.

The hummingbird hovers, wings beating frantically to disintegration, a monosyllabic noise, because we are curious about one another.

I want to make something of myself in the water, fish nudging me, but I keep losing myself.

I'm watching a crow fly far in the chilly weather. Whose sky is it?

I pick up a hard-shelled insect from a used plate in my kitchen and place it back outside.

I see the bear roaming a Montana hillside. I'm glad for the distance between us.

The frog's body fills with noise, releases it like a girl who has put her packages down.

I unscientifically come to a precipice to see what the eagle sees.

The suspicious elk, embedded in a contagious darkness, worries about the unreliable things moving around him.

I want to make something out of something else.

"Species dysphoria" affects people who believe they were born in the wrong species and can feel phantom limbs, claws, tails, or wings. They are creatures trapped in a human body. They think about flying, burrowing, swimming, jumping, climbing, and running, so that they can leave their shapes and shadows behind. They can be too large or awkward playing with balls or balloons, ascending stairs or ladders, fetching a necklace or chewing on it. Or so small they want to believe they can fit through a mouse hole or the space beneath a door. Ceilings and floors know nothing. These people reuse their hands, mouths, feet. An open window changes its meaning. Relevance is learned from swallowing clouds and depositing them at the feet of the woman who calls you home using your pet name. This is a place you like, with goat hearts beating under the moon, inviting grass to sway, hiding behind a ropey tree, twisting toward light. Evening seems more important than morning when you are mindless and tired and the landscape is full of relevant gestures. You rehearse who you are, someplace you are welcomed.

I gather beauty, which sometimes thinks only about itself and, if collected and seen in the right way, inspires joy, as if there could possibly be more beauty. But to get there, I need to be as reckless as a beast, enjoy the possible and move forward. I need to watch for dogs that swarm menacingly from a periphery, refocus on my intrusive illusions, and my unlovable ideas. My mind trespasses through the broken window of a house to discover what is precious on someone else's desk, a heart packed in ice, a story set against the animal kingdom. Mine is the same window, house, and desk. We are all related although we see things differently, through the kaleidoscope of our various experiences. Some of the things I imagine do happen, like seeing pelicans excited about fish, a smoldering fire on a beach on a winter night, stars smiling as darkness arrives, the radio reciting. I'm always alone although there are sometimes people around me, my husband and a friend or two, and animals, especially animals. I'll always ask why. I'll always be shocked and amazed by the world. I need to wonder what happens without exactly knowing why or who. Who will change? We can talk about that, too.

# The Etiquette of Space

# The Etiquette of Space

I need an emptiness around me which makes it easier to move. Unencumbered, I go in any direction and still go nowhere. This is a time before covid-19. A room in my Seattle house or a spot on a winter beach resembles Iceland without its vast frozen ground. I'm unlimited but I'm unburdened, wearing only the weight of clothes and gravity. Time seems suspended. Everything around me is slow and full, ocean waves. A truck, filled with televisions, passes. I'm reading through a stack of letters, thumbing through sophisticated family photographs while sitting in a kind of chair that swivels everywhere like instinct. I breathe space in and out and therefore my body is partially composed of space. As I try to grow lighter, walking down the beach, I see two teenagers rubbing against each other awkwardly under a tree near the duck and turtle pond. Sand shifts their limbs, engulfing parts of their bodies not marooned on a blanket. While their friction is unappealing, I can't look away from them.

People who need to be touched are like people enthusiastically buying appliances using credit. They describe what they desire and plumb their emotional depths to pay. It's called "skin hunger" in psychological terms, people who need people around them, not necessarily touching them. They are often avoiding something about themselves, the way a strange household sound startles someone, but they gravitate to it since it interrupts their sad thoughts. All their dramatic moments are shared and dispersed, bees entertained by the same piece of rotting fruit. I once took care of a neighbor's autistic boy, who grew into an autistic man. He disliked being touched, for a haircut or dental exam, or kissed or hugged. It was overwhelming.

I lived in "Big Sky Country," Missoula, Montana for about ten years, where labyrinthine mountains, rivers and lakes splurged with fish, and the sky spreading out over everything contained clouds, airplanes, rain, snow, sunshine. I could speed down an empty highway for quite a while, on the wrong side of the road. Houses suspiciously showed themselves every so often, peeking out surreptitiously from behind trees or bushes or fences. Cattle occasionally crossed the road in their sighing and sluggish manner, birds flitted overhead. Sometimes I caught the swagger of a coyote or grey wolf. In Seattle, where I live now, houses are springing up fast and I discover my moral resistance. The city is preoccupied with modernity and more, while nodding at nostalgia. You are spinning wildly alone in space, arms akimbo, and someone suddenly appears in front of you.

Isn't space an assemblage? Air, time, atoms and molecules different from mine, light, dark, elements. Space is distance, zooming in and out with a camera and finding the right length away in order to capture a picture. The future, past, and present are all parts of any photograph as well as space. And claustrophobia is a fear of small areas, which reminds me of an opinion that squeezes me into a corner. With claustrophobia, I can't change or escape, which I've felt inside the gondola of a Ferris wheel, which also triggered my fear of heights.

We too can be far from each other, my husband and me. People can be in emotional transition, yet outwardly nothing changes. But we always manage to come together, help one another. I will fill some open spaces by shouting nonsense at strangers in passing cars, covering holes in my rugs with cat toys, papers, and books, and by pouring hot tea over ice and snow. I hang and rehang paintings, moving close and then far away from them. In Seattle there are privately owned public spaces, mostly plazas with seating. Near one building downtown there's a tiny park near the water, with a locked fence. But there are still more and more buildings aimlessly rising in front of me.

With space you can believe there's nothing more to discover, but I can stand at my window for hours. Outside, a candy wrapper throws itself up and down the street, a loose dog hesitates, deciding where to go, and a child in ballet flats hurries down the sidewalk. Some days I want to be seen. I want to engulf all that space, be noticed and greeted. While evolutionary wheat fields or older houses are bulldozed to create our new complicated lives, I determine what subcultural things to write on a blank piece of paper. We are so many contradictory things contained in the small space of ourselves.

Recitative spaces:
disappointed squirrels thrust themselves through summer soil
an accomplished fire punctuates night
unlocked complaints roll around inside a mouth
a compliant sky always waits to be rearranged
a door opens up spilling someone new into the room
in sleep I can go anywhere in my dream train
somewhere there is a revolution with people staining the streets
air identifies the words clouding it
one season collects all the things it can then releases them, changed, in the next season
something scurries away from me on the lawn

I visited Iceland this winter. Because it was so cold and there was an abundance of space, I needed to "suit up" when I went outside. Outer space is defined as a void without boundaries between celestial bodies, with a sprinkling of low density particles, mainly hydrogen gas, and the presence of electromagnetic radiation. (*Reference, "What is outer space made of?"*). There's too much dark matter, 27% of the energy and mass in the universe. It's undetectable and unknown. Dark energy, antigravity, is evidenced throughout outer space, constituting about 68%, and is theorized to enhance the expansion of the universe. (*Hubblesite, "What is dark energy"*).

Sometimes space is disguised and is actually something else, like water or a desert or a field of grass. I need space to expand. Japanese maples grown in a small space stay small. I can't. I'm slowly turning away from something/someone who finally wants me.

There is another space in my bathtub. There are spaces for several people in my yard. There is space in my living room if I remove all the furniture and clutter. There is enough space on the sidewalks between houses, buildings, and cars. I live in the augmenting of Seattle, which is limited by water on several sides. Most places have special functions, bedroom = leisure, kitchen = food, movie theatre = movies, tennis court = tennis, bicycle shop = bicycles, bookstore = solitude. But it is fun to mix them up, bedroom = tennis, kitchen = solitude, tennis court = movies etc. Sometimes this happens naturally. If you never leave someplace, then you are always "here." You can disappear as easily in the city as the forest.

The sidewalks and streets under my feet grow smaller and smaller as I leave them behind. They are specimens of cement winding all around the city in long, continuous rectangles, surrounding other areas and structures. Indoors people are aware of the placement of objects, a wooden table arranged with photographs, vases, and books that rearrange the gaps between bodies or objects.

I have little pity for my new stray cat since he goes places I don't know anything about. The hidden parts of our yards and homes are tenuous and frightening, migrating shrubs, rusted tools, worn wood fences, broken walls, decrepit basements and abandoned houses. These are the places we hate to enter to search for something lost or because there is some strange noise, the inconvenient, hysteria-inducing spots. Many people keep themselves hidden because they try to recreate themselves using media images and expectations or because they have stuffed too much inside and don't want it to escape or because they don't trust themselves. And if we see that something is covered, in a shed, in a box, with slightly revealing clothing, under a pillow, behind someone's back, under plastic or some delicious or fermenting food in a container inside the refrigerator, the mystery makes us curious. I used to hide behind the front door when my husband was coming home, and I enjoyed leaping out and scaring him. The more of a surprise it was, the more fun it was. Finally he coaxed me into stopping, saying, "I'm going to have a heart attack."

Dealing with surprises means I'm growing up. I surprised myself by crying and hoping my husband would marry me a week before our wedding when he decided that I had been right all along in saying that I was too old for him. Now we've been married nearly thirty years. There are abandoned rituals and naturally evolving occurrences to which I mumble, "Oh!" But it's the external events and spontaneous crises that can change me, national elections or someone with a deeply disturbing face walking menacingly toward me, or a joyous impulse to drive to the beach. Children like changes but not sudden shocks. My cat, that mostly lived his life outdoors, still startles at the tiniest noises, often ones I can't hear. I'm very careful with sharp objects or potential weapons. I appropriate my husband for a moment when I frighten him. His mind is empty, and he's totally mine for that brief minute when his thoughts aren't elsewhere.

Our worlds are usually predictable and there's a giant inflated white plastic polar bear positioned on a nearby front lawn, wearing red mittens and a red hat, nestled among strings of lights and clumps of pine branches arranged in circles. Somewhere else, bombs generously explode, broken people break things, wars creep past borders, accidents occur, religions are born and then die. Time embraces us all, digging its fingers into our flesh.

The problem with space and direction: in Rome I planned to visit a certain monument but became lost among the diagonal, mythical streets and ended up at another equally immortal and enjoyable monument. In Rome I spoke to the river and fountains, asking for directions, but they didn't answer me. Lost, I felt alone, stuck with myself.

When I was young, my mother would tell me to go play outside. Our family spent summers beyond New York City and a few were spent near long reluctant beaches on Long Island. When she took some baby chicks away from me, I angrily began a long clumsy walk down a road that eventually ran, like an argument, toward a hut that served the local residents drinks with tiny umbrellas and tuna fish sandwiches. I didn't get lost, but I had adventures along the way. It was between lunch and dinner when I arrived there, not really thinking about a destination, more about escape. I had too much internal architecture that was churning. The owner sat me on a stool, a tiki bar top between us. He gave me a glass of water and said, "I'll call your pretty mother to come and pick you up." He winked at me. "Put in a good word for me." I stared at him from the straggly, tired, and thirsty bush of my body.

To truly become lost is to relinquish your spatial whereabouts, to be astray and adrift physically and mentally, unable to find your path, to be helpless, or, in the extreme, when something or someone can no longer be retrieved. I remembered the chicks chirping in the high grass around our rented house, and, as I approached, their twig legs ran away from me like errant ideas. Being lost is being deceived, on a nameless, numberless street, in an unknown country, abandoned in a forest where everything looks the same, not being able to figure out where you are because the bodies of others around you have moved.

To lose myself, I need to dissolve.

I watch a woman at the edge of a lake: about to dive, thinking, listening, studying.

I was waiting for words I couldn't locate.

Would you give yourself completely to an unidentified city?

Now I'm moving in several directions at the same time.

In the same large lake there is a mattress, a bicycle wheel, a plaid shirt sleeve, broken things, objects that slowly float to the surface or disappear entirely.

# What is Still Seen

# What Is Still Seen

Clouds, then a moon. A boat is going round and round aimlessly on a lake. Rain comes and goes, a curtain closing and opening. A woman is alone in the boat.

If she's not seen, does she matter?

Windows are filled with a tea-colored sky. A hawk thrusts loose, stitching the horizon. It catches something cacophonous and small, then drops it.

Does all that available space fill you?

A carousel is bobbing with children in a park. Laughter. Tree leaves are falling to the rhythm of the up and down motion, floating as if they are on a mechanical river.

Do the parents laugh too?

Morning, a man is asleep in a bed. The evening before a woman read a book to him. Now she is sitting in a chair, watching him twitch to his dreams.

Should she wake him or keep herself hidden?

The elderly woman is looking at photographs in an album, thinking about how people and places used to look. She remembers certain gestures over and over again.

Is this the same as life?

At the track, horses snort and stamp, waiting to enter the circle they will gallop through several times. People along the side consult programs and watch money's watery life changing.

Is this beauty with a purpose?

The woman kneels as stained glass windows stare at her. She is thinking about hate and love and miracles amid the singing. She closes her eyes, clasps her hands.

Is this helpful?

The cat stays in the yard, near the woman, tasting and smelling springtime. The cat's gestures are small. He is old and eases lopsidedly to the ground to sleep. The woman wants to do the same.

They see the beauty in one another.

The woman turns away from the man with a fire-gnawed face. It is a surprise she notices at a far restaurant table. She talks to her friends, touching her own face without thinking.

 Does someone still love him?


 The woman's mind is shrinking. The fog she lives in encompasses people, houses, events, conversations. Her new world is lovely and messy.

 Does it matter whether it's real or not?